W9-ATZ-523

4.95

THE
CHILCOTIN WAR

A Tale of Death and Reprisal

RICH MOLE

VICTORIA · VANCOUVER · CALGARY

Copyright © 2009 Rich Mole

All rights reserved. No part of this publication may be reproduced, stored in a retrieval system or transmitted in any form or by any means—electronic, mechanical, audio recording or otherwise—without the written permission of the publisher or a licence from Access Copyright, Toronto, Canada.

Heritage House Publishing Company Ltd.
heritagehouse.ca

Library and Archives Canada Cataloguing in Publication
Mole, Rich, 1946–
    The Chilcotin War: a tale of death and reprisal / Rich Mole.

(Amazing stories)
Includes bibliographical references and index.
ISBN 978-1-894974-96-7

    1. Chilcotin Indians—Wars—British Columbia. 2. Chilcotin Indians—and tenure—History. 3. Klatsassin, d. 1864. 4. Waddington, Alfred, 1800?–1872. 5. British Columbia—History—1849–1871. I. Title. II. Series: Amazing stories (Surrey, B.C.)

E99.T78M64 2009   971.1'02   C2009-904501-X

Series editor: Lesley Reynolds.
Cover design: Chyla Cardinal. Interior design: Frances Hunter.
Cover photo: Sketch of Homathko Canyon, Bute Inlet (most likely by Frederick Whymper), as it appeared in *The Illustrated London News*, September 5, 1868, Sunfire Publications Collection. Interior photos: British Columbia Archives, page 13 (A-01885); page 21 (C-06116); page 31 (A-04656); page 44 (A-01454); page 72 (I-68446); page 97 (A-01752); page 121 (A-01127); page 133 (A-08953). Chilcotin map: Rob Struthers, Dennis & Struthers Visual Communications Inc.

The interior of this book was produced using 100% post-consumer recycled paper, processed chlorine free and printed with vegetable-based inks.

Heritage House acknowledges the financial support for its publishing program from the Government of Canada through the Canada Book Fund (CBF), Canada Council for the Arts and the province of British Columbia through the British Columbia Arts Council and the Book Publishing Tax Credit.

18 17 16 15 2 3 4 5
Printed in Canada

Contents

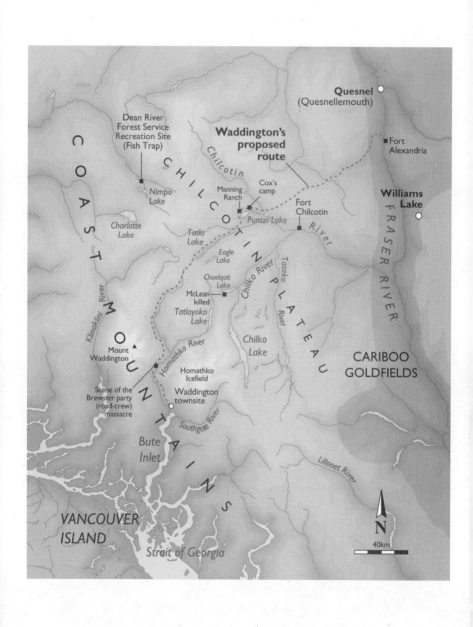

Quesnel
(Quesnellemouth)

Fort
Alexandria

Williams
Lake

Dean River
Forest Service
Recreation Site
(Fish Trap)

Waddington's
proposed
route

C O A S T

C H I L C O T I N

Nimpo
Lake

Manning
Ranch

Cox's
camp

Fort
Chilcotin

Chilcotin

Puntzi Lake

River

F R A S E R   R I V E R

Charlotte
Lake

Tatla
Lake

Eagle
Lake

Choelqoit
Lake

McLean
killed

Tatlayoko
Lake

Chilko River

Chilko
Lake

Toseko
River

P L A T E A U

CARIBOO
GOLDFIELDS

Klinaklini   River

Mount
Waddington

M O U N T A I N S

Homathko   River

Homathko
Icefield

Scene of the
Brewster party
(road-crew)
massacre

Waddington
townsite

Bute
Inlet

Southgate   River

Lillooet River

VANCOUVER
ISLAND

Strait of Georgia

N

40km

Author's Note

The story of the Chilcotin War is an epic of exploration and the quest for gold. It is also a violent tale of obsession, greed and a fatal clash of cultures. The war was a tragedy, and many people in British Columbia still live in its shadow.

In retelling this dramatic story, I have relied on the testimony of those who either experienced the events or listened to those who had. A Tsilhqot'in manhunt volunteer scribbled in his diary the words he was told legendary Donald McLean spoke minutes before he was killed. A Hudson's Bay Company (HBC) trader made a detailed entry in his record book about a Native attack on Fort Alexandria, providing valuable clues about why the independent Tsilhqot'in had little use for the white man's trade. BC's fearful, frustrated new governor, Frederick Seymour, poured out his anguish to colonial officials in London. In 1861, entrepreneur

Alfred Waddington listened to Robert Homfray's tales of near-death at Bute Inlet and decided to hide what he had heard. We know because 30 years later Homfray finally confessed that he had agreed to keep silent.

Many bore witness to the tragedy and told of their experiences: to Judge Begbie in his frontier courtroom; to an Anglican priest in a stinking log jail; to a newspaper reporter inside a Victoria hospital ward; to a humiliated war chief who feared for his people; and to an incredulous police chief who buried bodies and marvelled at the folly of misguided men.

Those involved had their own individual perceptions and biases. We cannot always be certain that they got it right. Despite the many eyewitness accounts, sometimes author-detectives must make assumptions based on a careful reading of the evidence. This author-detective owes much to others, chief among them former Kamloops newspaper editor Mel Rothenburger—Donald McLean's great-grandson—whose Chilcotin War narratives showed the way.

Since the 1860s, our attitudes have changed. Contemporary language reflects those changes. In the 1800s, almost everyone called the indigenous peoples of North America "Indians" or "savages." The former term reflected Columbus' geographical error and was often used without malice. Before human rights became an accepted concept, most people held attitudes now thought discriminatory, and even those considered highly principled and God-fearing casually used words we now regard as erroneous and derogatory. Such words and attitudes appear in these pages in the interest of historical accuracy, and the author intends no disrespect.

Prologue

CREW FOREMAN WILLIAM BREWSTER *swung his hatchet, sending bark whirling over the precipice to the river hidden below and revealing a bright patch of white spruce wood. A clearly blazed trail meant there would be no mistaking the route when the crew came up to chop trees, clear brush and blast rock for the new roadbed.*

Carving Alfred Waddington's road up the Homathko Canyon and through the mountains to provide prospectors with a shortcut to Cariboo gold took everything the crew had: axes and shovels, drills and dynamite and, most of all, the sweat and strain of hard-working men driven to finish this stretch of the road by summer's end.

In the wilderness solitude, the ominous metallic clack that caught Brewster's ears seemed louder than it actually was. He knew that sound; it was a musket's heavy hammer falling on flint. But there was no answering explosion, no impact from a musket ball to send him sprawling into the rainforest undergrowth.

Misfire.

Brewster whirled around, eyes wide.

"Who is it?" he shouted.

"We have killed the others and we are going to kill you!" a voice yelled back.

"Why would you want to kill me?" Brewster asked, knowing the answer. He and his crew had invaded the territory of the Tsilhqot'in (Chilcotin) people. Instinctively, Brewster began to stumble in the direction of the other three men who made up the road crew's advance party.

The reply to Brewster's question came from the unseen musket: a bright flash, blue-white smoke and a musket ball he heard whistle past his face. The foreman turned and ran for his life. In the distance, more shots split the wilderness silence.

CHAPTER

1

The Lure

INSIDE FORT VICTORIA, JAMES DOUGLAS fingered the gold nugget. A Shuswap Native had lifted it off the bank of the Thompson River, 400 kilometres away. Donald McLean, HBC chief trader at Fort Kamloops, had shown good sense in writing so quickly about the find and sending along the proof. The governor of Vancouver Island reached for his quill. He wanted to give McLean instructions right away. Get as much gold as you can; encourage the Shuswap to dig for it, Douglas wrote, although he knew rich strikes would doom the fur trade. Recalling the chaos of the recent California gold rush, Douglas feared the worst. How long could the company keep the discoveries quiet?

As more gold nuggets and dust arrived at Fort Victoria,

the answer was obvious: not long. Victoria had no mint to convert the gold to bars or coins. Having no other choice, Douglas ordered 800 ounces of gold ore loaded onto HBC's *Otter* for the short trip south to San Francisco.

The Visionary Wholesaler

San Francisco had been the heart of the California gold rush, but by 1858 times were tough. Banks had closed. People were out of work. There was no way to keep the arrival of *Otter*'s golden cargo a secret. The news spread northeast to the Sacramento Valley, gold rush "ground zero," where former forty-niners worked as gold-company wage slaves. Here was their second chance. Unstaked gold lay just three days' travel north. Men dashed downriver and across the bay to board a boat—any boat—bound for this island called "Vancouver."

It wasn't just would-be prospectors who were excited. Businessmen, including wholesale grocer Alfred Waddington, knew that gold finds on the Fraser River could mean big business. Prospectors needed to eat, didn't they? Despite the promise of profit, skeptics doubted Waddington's wisdom in leaving the comforts of San Francisco for the dreary hardships of a wilderness outpost.

Close to 60, Waddington had already outlived many of his generation and was regarded as an old man. Yet the aristocratic British-born entrepreneur scarcely gave his age a thought. Waddington's upper-class demeanour hid the heart of an adventurer. A decade before, upon hearing news of California gold discoveries, Waddington had abandoned a comfortable life managing a French steel mill and his family's cotton mills, bade stunned relatives goodbye and sailed away to seek his second fortune. Now he was off again.

Within minutes of plunging into the jostling wharfside crowd, the visionary wholesaler was aboard one of the dozens of overcrowded paddlewheelers that had been pressed into service for the new rush to riches. Waddington's destination was not yet a bustling gold-rush town. He found Victoria "a quiet village" of a few hundred residents, with no gold whatsoever. Victoria was merely the closest port to the gold-laden Fraser River sandbars, which lay across the unpredictable waters of the Strait of Georgia. Within a few weeks, many of the American newcomers were already heading home. "We hear every day that Victoria has caved in," Waddington complained, "that the gold mines are a humbug; that our soil is poor, the climate Siberian; that Victoria is no port at all and that the city will have to be removed somewhere else; in short, that the bubble has burst."

This was not the vibrant business environment Waddington had expected. That had to change. First, he needed to discover where the gold was and what it took to get it. He learned that reaching the gold was much more difficult than actually getting it out of the ground. The first finds on the lower Fraser had disappeared quickly, and gold seekers were venturing farther inland. By summer's end, a paddlewheeler was churning up Harrison Lake on the first leg of the prospectors' weeks-long trek to the upper Fraser. When steamer passengers disembarked, there was no easy road to riches. In fact, there was no road at all.

Waddington was further incensed when he learned that Governor Douglas had personally persuaded 500 men to work on a lakehead trail and had them deposit $25 for the privilege! Their pay was credit on purchases made at the HBC store. The farther prospectors trudged, the higher the prices they paid. A pound of beans that cost 1.5 cents in Victoria fetched a dollar on the upper Fraser. "The whole thing can be explained by the conflicting struggles between free trade and monopoly," Waddington grumbled.

Waddington experienced first-hand the HBC's stranglehold on real estate. Abandoning the pretext of expanding the wholesale business, he bought up as many newly surveyed lots as the tight-fisted HBC allowed. Purchasers were limited to just four lots; nevertheless, Waddington soon amassed dozens of properties, buying more lots from those down on their luck. When the lots' gold-rush values spiralled up over 3,000 percent, his fortune was made.

A fort printer was astonished when Waddington handed him a heavy manuscript to run through his little press. This was no pamphlet—this was a book, the first the colony had ever published. Waddington's motivation for writing *The Fraser Mines Vindicated* wasn't literary; it was mercenary. Gold's lure was no illusion, Waddington told his readers in San Francisco and Sacramento. Riches were waiting.

Alfred Waddington's potentially profitable and time-saving road to Cariboo gold would cost him everything: money, property and reputation.

Brothers-in-Arms

One of those in Victoria who read *The Fraser Mines Vindicated* was another California free enterpriser. Some time before, the bright-eyed, bearded man in a frock coat and top hat had been plain Bill Smith, but when Smith shook hands with Waddington, he introduced himself as Amor De Cosmos. The two men were immediately drawn to one another. De Cosmos was the flamboyant, fiery-tempered pontificator whom Waddington perhaps wished he could be.

De Cosmos must have been attracted to Waddington's risk-taking intellect and keen perception.

De Cosmos' name might have puzzled the prospectors, but to a literate man such as Waddington, the blend of French, Latin and Greek was no mystery. It meant "love of the universe." But De Cosmos himself was a bit of a cipher. The former photographer of mining claims never said why he had changed his name or left California. It was clear, however, what he wanted to do on Vancouver Island: find his fortune. Like Waddington, De Cosmos did so without lifting a pick or pan. Within weeks of arriving, he, too, was a landowner.

The two men watched as the drama of gold-rush California was played out again. By July, the island colony's population had swollen to 6,000: "Polish Jews, Italian fishermen, French cooks, jobbers, speculators of every kind," Waddington wrote, along with "a fair seasoning of gamblers and swindlers, thieves, drunkards and jailbirds."

Most of the colonists shrugged off what Waddington called the HBC's "mean, despotic dealings," but property-owner Waddington had a stake in changing the status quo. De Cosmos also fumed about the oppressive HBC establishment and the colony's little seven-member House of Assembly. Late one fall evening, over drinks in the rear of the colony's new pharmacy, De Cosmos, Waddington and other businessmen established a weekly newspaper, the *British Colonist*. On December 11, 1858, the same press that had printed *The Fraser Mines Vindicated* was cranking out the first edition. Two weeks later, the *British Colonist* was demanding "the immediate establishment of self-govern-ment." By February, De Cosmos was declaring that "the man who will not ask Her Majesty's Government to remove Governor Douglas is a traitor to his country."

For Alfred Waddington, the newspaper De Cosmos founded proved to be far more useful than *The Fraser Mines Vindicated*. Because the two men's sentiments were so similar, De Cosmos printed Waddington's opinions and ideas regu-larly. In fact, the *British Colonist* began raising Waddington's profile with its very first edition: De Cosmos filled the front page with two excerpts from Waddington's book.

Big Plans

The inland route that led to the biggest potential gold deposits was long and tortuous. Most travellers took a paddlewheeler up the Fraser as far as Fort Hope. From there, they began a 225-kilometre hike to Lillooet, much of it through the forbidding Fraser Canyon. Others reached Lillooet via the Harrison Lake route, a 184-kilometre ordeal. From Lillooet, it was 319 kilometres to HBC's Fort Alexandria. Waddington guessed that the trail would become longer as more men moved up into virgin territory. He was right. Less than two years later, thousands of prospectors would make an addi-tional 125-kilometre trip northeast from Fort Alexandria toward the richest gold-bearing earth of the newly united island-mainland colony of British Columbia.

By 1859, some began to speculate that there was a quicker, more profitable way to get men and supplies into what prospectors were calling Cariboo country: a route up one of the coastal inlets. Because Victoria would become the embarkation point for a quick voyage up the Strait of Georgia, town merchants immediately endorsed the idea. Disembarking at the head of some inlet, paying prospectors and profitable pack trains would simply wind their way through the mountains into easily travelled Chilcotin territory and then amble east to Fort Alexandria, on the opposite side of the Fraser River. A short steamboat ride upriver would put them all within a day or two of creeks loaded with gold. But which inlet offered the best potential route?

James Douglas sent Major William Downie to explore the possibilities. Downie heard from Natives that Bute Inlet was navigable. The river through the Cascade Mountains above it was called Pryce River, or the Homathko, after the tribe living on Bute Inlet. The river also appeared to be navigable, although Downie never saw either waterway himself.

Then Waddington met Mark Bate. A Nanaimo HBC agent, Bate had sent an expedition into the inlet to pre-empt some land for settlement, but abandoned his plans. Nevertheless, what little Waddington heard from Bate was enough. He would build a toll road from Bute Inlet through the mountains and across the Chilcotin Plateau to the Fraser and get rich on the dreams of Cariboo prospectors.

2

Keeping the Dream Alive

BY LATE 1859, AMOR DE COSMOS was publishing his former weekly five days a week. Waddington's bowling saloon and business leases were making the entrepreneur wealthy. As their personal fortunes and public profiles grew, both men continued to rail at the colonial government's inefficiencies —De Cosmos through his newspaper and Waddington through a second book, but it wasn't enough for either.

Both ran as candidates in the 1860 general election. De Cosmos was defeated for appearing as a drunken braggart. (He suffered a second defeat due to by-election confusion when he was forced to run under his real name, Smith, rather than De Cosmos.) Waddington won a seat in the House of Assembly, but it was not a happy time. Backing politically unpopular causes—including a successful bill to prevent the sale of intoxicants to Natives—Waddington often feuded with flamboyant and corrupt Attorney General George Cary.

Meanwhile, prospectors continued to head for the Cariboo. That summer, a group of intrepid gold seekers left the crowds behind and headed northeast, just as Waddington had predicted they would. At remote Antler Creek, they found gold so close to the surface they didn't even have to dig for it. But the trails these men travelled were still long and difficult, and Waddington still dreamed of offering a quick and profitable route to the gold creeks through Bute Inlet.

William Downie scoffed. "None of us will ever see a wagon road from Bute Inlet to the Fraser," he told the New Westminster–based *British Columbian*. Others on the mainland agreed. De Cosmos dismissed them as "a clique of discontented men with no money and less brains."

By the summer of 1861, Governor Douglas couldn't ignore the growing enthusiasm whipped up by Waddington and De Cosmos. He dispatched Downie up the coast. A few weeks later, the Major was back in Victoria.

The Scheme Unfolds

In smoke-filled Moore's Hall, Downie gazed down from the stage at an impatient audience of 250 people. Victoria had been buzzing with speculation ever since his return. A road? Fine, but perhaps there was gold up at Bute!

Downie noticed Amor De Cosmos and Alfred

Waddington. He knew that they were not going to like what they were about to hear. He gestured toward the large maps and told the audience about his attempts to find a passage through the mountains, first at Bute Inlet, then up at Bella Coola. Taking the "very dangerous" trek up the main river ("the Hermatsker"), Downie reported the perpendicular mountains became more formidable as they climbed higher. He described the trail above Bentinck Arm as passing through "the most miserable terrain I have seen in British Columbia. The mountains ran straight up and down. Not even a bear trail is visible. And where a bear can't get along, there's a poor show for a wagon road." Indian trails to the coast? Perhaps, but no available trail could be opened up. The country was too rough for cheap packing, or any packing at all, he said.

The crowd didn't like this. "What's he talking about?" someone jeered.

"Put him out!" another shouted.

Something thumped onto the stage. A lantern crashed to the hall floor. Dodging the missiles arcing in his direction, Downie wouldn't be cowed. "I have seen nothing on the inlet to justify any man in spending money or time in going there," he shouted.

Was agriculture, fishing or logging possible at Bute? De Cosmos asked. Lots of salmon, Downie told the editor, but the soil and timber were too light for farming or logging. And forget about finding the motherlode. Downie told the crowd there probably wasn't enough gold on the entire coast to pay a man a dollar a day. At a time when many Cariboo prospectors were digging up $20 to $100 a day, that may have been the worst news—not only for would-be prospectors, but for Waddington and De Cosmos as well.

The two men dismissed Downie's inlet exploration as superficial. Waddington felt he had to see Bute Inlet for himself. Like Californians years before, some Victoria citizens must have questioned his sanity. If Downie couldn't get through, how was an old man going to manage it? Besides, didn't he have obligations to the Assembly?

Waddington likely shrugged off these concerns. At worst, he would only miss a session or two; the Assembly only met each Thursday. (As Waddington learned when he returned from the inlet, so many members were cheering on their favourites at the Beacon Hill racetrack that on two occasions the House couldn't reach a quorum and no business was done at all.) Besides, here was an opportunity to escape George Cary's snide asides and avoid appearing like an old fool.

* * *

High above the place where the Homathko River emptied itself into the Bute Inlet, blue-black mountains brooded over the tiny steamer *Henrietta* as it chugged along the winding waterway. Filled with excitement, Alfred Waddington gazed in awe at peaks crested with a glistening mantle of snow.

Later that day, crew members nudged the steamer's boat into the bank near the head of the inlet. The land seemed

Newspaper editor Amor De Cosmos regarded
Alfred Waddington as a kindred spirit. Both
men abhorred the autocratic HBC's control
of business.

to swallow up the tiny group. Enormous bluffs draped with
thick, dark moss loomed overhead. Hidden cliffs rose up
behind a tangle of twisted trees and dripping deadfalls.
Following the river, the group climbed steadily for days.
Panting and perspiring, the young men of the party
marvelled at how the old man kept going.

Silent, half-naked men with rings through their noses led the way. After initial suspicion, their gaze was unflinching, their step along the slanting pathway purposeful and assured—so different from the beaten, cowed Natives around Victoria, Waddington must have noted. Through signs and gestures, they had told him more than he had hoped. Yes, there was a trail. More than 25 kilometres up the river, Waddington left a party of five men with, as he reported later, "level country ahead of them."

As the steamer made its way back to the inlet's mouth, Waddington's plan was likely already taking shape. The passing silhouette of the forest would be replaced by a wharf, sturdy cabins and stores. On the south shore, a harbour and townsite would take shape. He would buy up as much land as he could and persuade others to invest. He had to determine tolls on the road. First, however, he would write a full report for the governor—another exploration was needed. And Victoria must know the facts. He would turn again to Amor De Cosmos.

"A route has been discovered," the *British Colonist* crowed a few days after Waddington's return. "There is no insurmountable obstacle in the way."

Fighting for Survival

Four months later, Robert Homfray paused to gaze down Bute Inlet. Numb and exhausted, the civil engineer was thankful that he and his six companions were still alive. When Homfray had accepted James Douglas' offer to lead

Waddington's 1861 Bute Inlet exploration, others thought him mad. A voyage that was dangerous in the summer would be even more hazardous in October. Few expected to see him alive again. Homfray now concluded that the skeptics were probably right. He and the others were likely doomed.

Yet, he had thought the same days before, when six Natives in a war canoe had pursued them and taken them prisoner. The timely arrival of a Klahoose chief had saved them. His terrorizing war whoops had sent the others paddling frantically off into the mist. The group owed their lives to the fact that the chief had thought Homfray was friendly Alfred Waddington, whom he had met during his recent trip.

The chief repeated what he had told Waddington. A trail existed through the mountains. However, snow now blocked the way. But Homfray would not be dissuaded. The next day, the chief suddenly turned back, advising Homfray to do the same. Instead, the party struggled on through the river's numbing rapids. Friendly Tsilhqot'in took the frigid men to their subterranean houses, where Homfray heard the same story again. A trail existed, but snow made it impassable. He decided to give up.

With icy spray stiffening their clothes and numbing their legs and chests, the men fought to control their large Native canoe as it hurtled down the Homathko toward the inlet. Homfray's Native guides cried out a warning, but it came too late. With a bone-jarring impact, the canoe impaled itself upon the torn limb of a floating tree. Water began to gurgle around their knees.

Desperate hands reached out to the tree trunk and the men crawled onto the narrow, slippery surface. Their tents and food still lay in the canoe. Without them, there was no hope of survival. Homfray edged out to the half-submerged craft and snatched at the dripping sacks and bundles. The men hoisted Homfray across to the narrow trunk. Happily, the tree carried them to the riverbank. It was then that someone remembered the axes.

Homfray crawled out over the half-submerged canoe once again, one of his voyageurs close behind. Stretching down, he plunged his hands into the water that spilled over the craft and passed the axes to waiting hands above. Homfray heaved himself up onto the tree and watched the river rip the canoe apart and whirl it into the foam.

Four days later, the starving group tore through concealing brush to reach cached provisions. One of the guides managed to light a small fire. Outstretched hands trembled above the flames' feeble warmth. Looking up, one man nudged another wordlessly. Circling the small perimeter, gaunt wolves stared at the exhausted men until they were driven back with flaming firewood.

The men faced freezing or starvation without a boat to reach help. Axes in hand, Homfray and others walked into the forest. The third tree they chopped down hit the ground and remained intact. The men took turns cutting limbs away and hollowing out the log that remained. Ten days later, the group stood staring at their crude craft. "Then," Homfray related later, "nearly everyone refused to get on it."

A swell of any size on the inlet would surely capsize the log boat. In the freezing water, lives would be measured in mere minutes. The choice was stark: drown or starve.

Hugging the shoreline, the men cautiously paddled their makeshift canoe in the shallows, "expecting to go down at any moment," Homfray recalled. Hours later, safe on shore near the inlet's mouth, Homfray and two voyageurs watched the other four paddle out in the direction of Native villages, praying that they would return with help before the food supply ran out. Their prayers were answered sooner than Homfray had hoped, and within a few days Natives were paddling the party across open water to Vancouver Island, where farmers sped word of their imminent arrival in Victoria.

When Homfray and his group stumbled onto the wharf below the HBC stores, Alfred Waddington and company personnel hurried to meet them, stunned at the pathetic sight of the ragged men shuffling painfully up the planking.

Alone with Waddington, Homfray held nothing back, reciting the horrors and hardships they had endured. The Indians had confirmed the trail, then? Waddington asked. Homfray nodded, perhaps startled that the life-threatening trials he related seemed to make no impact. At the end of the meeting, Waddington asked Homfray to keep the details of his ordeal to himself. The zealous visionary *had* heard everything Homfray had said and now was asking him to keep his mouth shut about it. Homfray knew why. Alfred Waddington had important business interests to protect. It would be 30 years before Homfray would finally make the details of his horrific Bute Inlet experiences public.

* * *

Surveyor and road builder Herman Tiedeman put pen to paper: "Fort Alexandria, July . . . 1862." Tiedeman's words conveyed what the crudely drawn map attached to his official report to Alfred Waddington could not. The torturous travels his party had survived had been hell: "Sir. Reduced almost to a skeleton, unable to walk."

Weeks later, in Victoria, Waddington likely skipped over Tiedeman's narrative: "Starvation was nearly our destiny . . . our Indians deserted us . . . still a miracle how I escaped with my heavy bundle and gun on my pack." The surveyor had travelled along the entire Homathko River through the mountains to the plateau beyond. From the river's mouth to Big Lake (Tatlayoko), Tiedeman assured Waddington, "a wagon road can be easily constructed." From Tatlayoko to the Fraser River, the surveyor saw "beautiful country."

Living the Dream
Based on nothing more than hearsay and a hunch, Waddington had managed to persuade Governor Douglas to amend the agreement for a bridle trail to a more substantial wagon road.

Now, the entrepreneur felt vindicated. Tiedeman's report did more than give credence to Waddington's confident boasts. It provided the proof that potential investors needed. It was time to make the scheme official. With the support of De Cosmos and other Victoria business leaders, Waddington incorporated the Bute Inlet Wagon Road Company Limited.

By September, the sounds of saws, axes and hammers were echoing up Bute Inlet. A trail was being hewn out of the rugged wilderness. Two months later, Waddington arrived back in Victoria. There were handshakes and brave smiles. Thirty-seven kilometres of road had been constructed along the river. In that short distance, the workers had been forced to construct over 40 bridges. Now, winter weather had brought work to a close. The charter gave the company only a year to complete the road, but Waddington realized that an extension was crucial. Publicly, he smiled confidently. Privately, however, he must have frowned in despair. So many bridges needed, so little distance covered—just a little over halfway between the inlet head and the canyon.

As Tiedeman had struggled up the Homathko, explosions reverberated through the mighty Fraser Canyon to the south. Fifty-two Royal Engineers were dynamiting out a bed for a Cariboo road that would eventually stretch over 600 kilometres to the new gold camps of Richfield, Barkerville and Camerontown. Alfred Waddington now had a road-building rival—Governor Douglas himself. Soon, others would join the great "road race" to the Cariboo.

3

Road Rivals

ONE DAY IN THE EARLY fall of 1861, around the time Alfred Waddington was steaming back from his excursion to Bute Inlet, HBC's *Otter* pulled away from a New Westminster wharf. Along with outward-bound prospectors escaping the Cariboo cold for salubrious Victoria, the steamer carried $100,000 worth of gold, a staggering sum at a time when a labourer earned less than $400 a year.

The huge shipment should have made Waddington and his investors very happy men; however, a significant threat to their enterprise was emerging.

Unfair Competition

Alfred Waddington opened the *British Colonist* and stared.

There it was, in bold black type: "ONE THOUSAND LABOURERS ... TO WORK ON THE GREAT TRUNK ROAD FROM YALE TO CARIBOO." Waddington could only dream of a work party that large. It wasn't the first such advertisement placed by one of the government's road-building contractors.

The work gang that travelled up to Bute in the summer of 1862 numbered just 70 men, all that the new Bute Inlet Wagon Road Company could afford. Other costs were skyrocketing, and the government—his road-building competitor—had its hand out, too, for fees and filing charges.

Meanwhile, the government was hiring all the contractors it wanted for its own Fraser Canyon road-building project. In turn, contractors hired all the men they needed. "Spare no expense" was not a phrase used openly, but with thousands of prospectors on the trail, the government's objective was clear: get the road built as quickly as possible. It didn't matter that the colonial government didn't have the money; Douglas could ask the home government in England for the funds. The Cariboo Road amounted to unfair competition.

Some other people in Victoria were already complaining, but not about government unfairness. To Waddington's astonishment, their complaints were aimed at his own road. "We would advise the public if they appreciate a good hearty laugh, to view the map of the Bute Inlet route to the Cariboo," sneered the *Evening Press*, a *Colonist* competitor. "Mountains are levelled, valleys filled up and the Bute Route is at once made a Roman highway."

Waddington's vision provided a focal point for the long-simmering feud between Victoria and New Westminster. When De Cosmos had labelled Victoria's trading rival "a third-rate Indian village," readers chuckled. Now, the Bute Inlet scheme was "creating ill-feeling between the two colonies," worried islanders whined, and "getting all the Fraser River towns opposed to us." To Waddington and De Cosmos, these people were traitors in their midst.

Then, quite abruptly, Alfred Waddington resigned from the Assembly. As representatives wrangled over his resolution for a Victoria mint, he had left to relieve himself. On his way back, he unexpectedly met the gleeful Assembly members in the hallway. The group had taken advantage of his brief absence, adjourned the sitting and shelved his mint resolution. Waddington guessed their motive. The members had avoided the passage of his resolution and potential public outcry over mint construction and operation expenses.

Waddington was outraged and regarded their behaviour as a personal insult. Nevertheless, he may have admitted to himself (but certainly to no one else) that the episode was also a blessing in disguise. Now he could focus all his energies to punching through his Bute Inlet road as quickly as possible.

Rivals Across the Water

While negative Bute Inlet comments from fellow Vancouver Islanders maddened Waddington and De Cosmos, both men expected mainland criticism. The city on the Fraser did not

The *British Colonist*'s Wharf Street office. Waddington used Amor De Cosmos' newspaper to promote his Bute Inlet "shortcut" to Cariboo gold.

disappoint them. It wasn't easy to shrug off New Westminster anymore. The rival across the water had become an incorporated city, a legitimacy still denied to Victoria partly because Assembly members were busy playing the ponies at the very moment incorporation was before the House.

In 1860, Governor Douglas had declared Victoria a free port. The new status meant American goods would be unloaded at Victoria instead of bypassing the island and going to New Westminster. Victoria shippers would have a profitable business transferring goods across the strait to the Fraser River port. Fearful New Westminster business owners imagined their lucrative river traffic vanishing the moment the Bute Inlet toll road opened. They found a champion in John Robson, a newspaper editor just as feisty as De Cosmos.

In the pages of his *British Columbian,* Robson editorialized that the Bute Inlet scheme was concocted by "selfish property owners in Victoria." Knowledgeable men—the editor named Major Downie—"and all those who should be best judges in the matter, have no faith in this North coast route . . . We have nothing to fear."

All this acrimony made some mainland businessmen stop and think. Enterprising individuals read Waddington's optimistic words about a short route to the gold deposits with increasing interest. What prospector in his right mind would hump his heavy pack on a long, winding trail when he could take a relaxing steamer voyage up the coast? They also read about the boatloads of crewmen Waddington was sending up to Bute. Perhaps he might just be on to something.

Waddington's New Threat

As if two proposed routes to the Cariboo—Bute Inlet and the Fraser Canyon route—weren't enough, in 1862, the governor had encouraged another group seeking a road charter. Their proposed road to riches began up the distant North Bentinck Arm of Dean Channel, past the Native village on the Bella Coola River. It was so far north that the very idea left Waddington mystified. But like Waddington, the shareholders in the Bentinck Arm and Fraser River Road Company Limited saw a chance to make money.

Alexander McDonald, a Chilcotin Plateau pack-train operator, knew both routes well. A former member of Downie's Bute expedition, he had later snowshoed through the mountains and down the Homathko River to the coast. Waddington was right; there was a route. But McDonald knew the proposed Bentinck Arm route even better. As for making money on the trail, Alex McDonald had a head start on everyone. McDonald and his partner, William Manning, had established a ranch in Chilcotin territory at Puntzi Lake, hundreds of kilometres from the nearest settlement. The ranch was a way station for pack-train crewmen and fellow travellers between Bella Coola and far-off Fort Alexandria. By 1862, McDonald's pack trains were already profitable.

While Waddington was attempting to sell shares and plan his first work season, his Bentinck Arm rival was reportedly negotiating with the HBC for the *Otter* to transport gold seekers to Bella Coola. "The nearest and cheapest way to Cariboo mines is by the Bentinck Arm Route," a front-page ad in Victoria's *Evening Press* announced. At Bella Coola, the ad continued, the Natives were "waiting to be of service to white men . . . willing to do anything."

Waddington must have been exasperated. When sea, lake and river navigation were taken into account, Bute was a shorter route than Bentinck by hundreds of kilometres! A comparison of land travel distances was even more favourable. Homathko River terrain was difficult, but, based on a recent official report, the Bentinck route appeared even more formidable.

In June 1862, Lieutenant H.S. Palmer had been sent up Bentinck Arm by Governor Douglas to survey a possible route. A slide area and steep precipice presented daunting barriers, the Royal Engineer reported. His journey to Fort Alexandria had taken 20 exhausting days. But nothing seemed to deter Bentinck backers, who kept work crews busy clearing brush for their proposed road.

Since the facts didn't seem to matter to his rivals or the critical public, Alfred Waddington decided to fight fire with fire. A few days after the Bentinck ad was published, another ad announced that the Bute Inlet Wagon Road Company had chartered a sloop to transport gold seekers and others on the first leg of Waddington's fast, efficient route to the Cariboo. At Bute Inlet, guides were waiting to take passengers to Fort Alexandria "through easily-travelled country."

At this early stage, Waddington must have hoped he'd have no takers. What mattered was public perception: anything Bentinck backers could do, Bute backers could do better. By the end of the summer, with only a few miles of road finished and a canyon yet to be conquered, Alfred Waddington was boasting that Fraser River pack trains moving through Bute Inlet would reach Fort Alexandria "in a week."

CHAPTER

4

The Victims

WHEN THE FEW PEOPLE WHO understood the Aboriginal peoples' plight read that the Nuxalk (Bella Coola) people were just "waiting to be of service to white men," they knew the northern Natives' motivation wasn't money. It was food. The Nuxalk were desperately hungry.

A poor run of fish in the inlets and rivers meant fewer fish in weirs and traps, fewer targets for pronged spears. Food shortages had also hit the Tsilhqot'in people farther south. They began to travel down to Bute Inlet more frequently, elbowing aside the Salish people at their traditional fisheries and increasing the competition for fish.

There were likely a number of environmental reasons why salmon weren't appearing as they once had.

Nevertheless, farther south on the Fraser, white newcomers were exacerbating the situation. These men weren't particularly awed by the seasonal spectacle of the salmon run, but they were certainly interested in its profit potential. Soon, they were using large nets to ensnare the fish. Natives had often given salmon away to starving visitors such as Herman Tiedeman and his party. Now, hungry themselves, they watched salmon being snatched up and sold to others.

Incursions by whites, first for furs, now for gold, meant the future of the Aboriginals was in doubt. Most Caucasians didn't care very much. The typical attitude was resignation. Some espoused Darwin's recent scientific "natural selection" theory, which they used to assuage any troublesome feelings of guilt. The dominant white race had always been destined to triumph over lesser races, they argued, citing 300 years of conquest throughout the Americas, from Peru to the Province of Canada. Events in the British colonies of Vancouver Island and British Columbia would soon seem to prove it once again.

Disease and Desperation

In mid-March 1862, a recently arrived prospector from San Francisco complained that he didn't feel well. A few days later, spots appeared on his face and chest. A diagnosis quickly confirmed what some had already guessed: the Victoria visitor had smallpox. The doctor who made the diagnosis didn't think it was a serious case.

Less than two weeks later, the *British Colonist* reported that some of the town's citizens had urged "the propriety of establishing a smallpox hospital." The story mentioned that smallpox had "already attacked" several children in the Songhees' harbour village. Whites often shook off the highly contagious disease or didn't contract it at all; a vaccine had been widely available for over 50 years. It was different for Natives.

Songhees chief Freezy knew that his village wasn't far enough away to protect them against the disease. Four years previously, his band had watched whites burn their earlier village to make way for streets and buildings. He didn't mind moving this time, though, and sought the isolation of a nearby island. Only his quick action saved the Songhees from the fate of another village on the outskirts of the town. This village was considered a breeding ground for the disease. Deaths had already been reported there, but villagers were reluctant to move. Three days after the Natives had ignored the order to evacuate, their huts were put to the torch. Homeless, the Natives now had no choice but to leave. They chose an ocean-front site called Ogden Point as their new home. It still wasn't far enough from the town to suit authorities.

Police were sent to Ogden Point to order the homeless people even farther north. Once the officers arrived, they quickly realized that not only hadn't the Natives moved far enough, they hadn't moved quickly enough, either. An overpowering stench of death greeted them. Unburied bodies lay where they had fallen. Knives, guns, tools and household articles had been left where their owners had dropped them. Officers later learned only a dozen had managed to flee northward in their canoes.

No doubt some felt the authorities' action regrettable, although they agreed that the close vicinity of the Natives had caused some social problems. A Committee of Nuisances had been struck to rid Humboldt Street of "houses of ill-fame" harbouring offensive Indian women with their "habitual drunkenness and disgusting language."

Nevertheless, the good citizens of Victoria were going to miss the convenience of Songhees and Haida peddlers who brought everything from grouse to moccasins to their doorsteps. And who was left to do the laundry? Only the Chinese with their mysterious ways. Two years before, Herman Tiedeman had hired Natives to do roadwork in front of the government offices. Where would builders find such cheap and convenient labour now?

Fire cleansed. In that respect, the village's destruction was regarded as something done for the Natives' own good—and for everyone else's, too. As the *British Colonist* put it, smallpox was "a scourge that may strike down our best citizens at any moment."

The homeless Natives paddled northward, "humanely taking their sick with them," the newspaper reassured its readers. No irony was intended, yet the decision to take the sick was hardly a humane one. Unwittingly, the travellers began to spread the scourge to other coastal tribes. Soon, the

Kwakwa̱ka'wakw, Coast Salish and Haida were dropping in delirium. Tens of thousands suffered hideous deaths.

A World Apart

After leaving Bella Coola, a small group of whites climbed the Bentinck Arm trail on their way to the Cariboo gold creeks. As they neared Anahim Lake, two in the party became so ill they could not go on. The large Tsilhqot'in village of Nancootlem seemed a convenient place to stop. The sick men slid off their mounts into the waiting hands of Tsilhqot'in women who led them inside one of their homes. The weary visitors likely didn't examine Nancootlem too closely. Still, what they saw may have surprised them.

The Tsilhqot'in were adept borrowers, adopting other First Nations' customs as their own. Nancootlem's substantial pole lodges—similar to the plank houses of the Nuxalk— were surrounded in part by a sturdy protective stockade. As winter approached, some southern Tsilhqot'in built circular subterranean pithouses (to which the Homfray party was taken), a type of home similar to that of the nearby Stl'atl'imx (Lillooet) people. Elsewhere on the plateau, the Tsilhqot'in constructed bark-and-branch huts, easily assembled by the semi-nomadic hunter-gatherers who wandered, mostly on foot, over bunchgrass hills and past poplar-dotted lakesides.

There were strong ties of marriage and trade between the Tsilhqot'in and the Nuxalk. Several times each year, the Tsilhqot'in travelled to the Nuxalk to hold council, to feast and dance and to honour the dead. Anahim, the village chief after whom the nearby lake was named, was a Nuxalk man who had taken a Tsilhqot'in wife.

To visiting whites, the Nancootlem villagers must have appeared far more primitive than the familiar coastal people they saw around New Westminster and Victoria. "Primitive" was how white people perceived Natives who didn't "put down roots," as many coastal peoples traditionally did for extended periods of time. "Savage" was another common term for those who had not adopted Christianity and at least some of the trappings of white civilization: clothing, weapons, cooking utensils and decorative gewgaws—the HBC's ubiquitous trade goods. Dressed in skins, furs and fang necklaces, adorned with ear or nose rings, paint and tattoos, how "savage" the Tsilhqot'in must have looked.

Another word frequently used to describe indigenous peoples was "treacherous," a term usually used in relation to warfare. It was an age in which opposing "civilized" armies still marched in close ranks to the rattle of drums on open, sunlit pastureland. By comparison, often silently stalking their foe after dark, the Tsilhqot'in would pounce suddenly on a sleeping enemy, a strategy practised for generations against the eastern Shuswap, western Homalco and especially the northern Carrier. Often both sides offered no quarter. Attacking a Carrier village when its chief was absent, the Tsilhqot'in killed all the children. The Carrier chief later retaliated, killing Tsilhqot'in youngsters.

The one people the Tsilhqot'in hadn't borrowed from were the whites. Coast Salish people had interacted with Europeans since the late 1700s, but the Tsilhqot'in had no first-hand knowledge of the newcomers until the 1820s. A particularly unnerving experience during Robert Homfray's Bute Inlet expedition— just a year before the white travellers stopped at Nancootlem—illustrates their isolation.

Homfray encountered a "tall, powerful Indian and his squaw" on the trail near the Homathko Canyon. Rushing up and embracing Homfray, the Tsilhqot'in then proceeded to give the expedition leader a close physical examination. "The Indian . . . looked into my mouth, examined my ears, to see if I were made like himself. He had evidently never seen a white man before."

Nor had these people any understanding of firearms. When one of Homfray's Native guides accidentally discharged his musket, "the half-naked Indians . . . had been so terribly frightened at the sudden report that they had all disappeared underground."

Meeting whites for the very first time, Homfray's Tsilhqot'in saviours were probably more curious than altruistic. On the plateau, they had already rejected these bizarre people and the peculiar things they treasured so much. Heavy iron pots? Closely woven spruce-root baskets were easier to carry and strong enough to hold hot rocks to heat water. Who would want a noisy, smoky musket? It was far better to quietly stalk deer or elk with a silent, swift *k'a* nocked on a bowstring. If the arrow missed, the hunter might take another shot or two before he was even noticed.

Few Tsilhqot'in understood English; most did not even speak the Chinook Jargon—a mélange of English, French and coastal Native tongues that was prevalent on the coast. Why learn the trade language when you had no use for the strangers' trade? The Tsilhqot'in usually put their own interests first, hunting for themselves rather than for exchange.

The HBC had been attempting to trade with the Tsilhqot'in off and on since 1821, when the Tsilhqot'in had invited the company to establish a plateau post. However, by the time tardy traders met the Tsilhqot'in, the Natives were wearing the warm pelts of the beaver they had originally killed for trade. After all, winter was approaching.

Five years later, the company earned the enmity of the Tsilhqot'in by harbouring a Carrier war party at Fort Alexandria. The Carriers brought in five Tsilhqot'in prisoners and proudly displayed the scalps of twelve others. Eighty Tsilhqot'in attacked the fort. Many were killed, and no doubt some were felled by muskets the traders had given the Carriers. After the Tsilhqot'in retreated, the Carriers tortured their prisoners and mounted their mutilated bodies on stumps for all to see.

No one had more experience with the Tsilhqot'in than Donald McLean. Some years before the chief trader sent that fateful gold nugget to James Douglas, he was put in charge of two plateau trading posts, including Fort Chilcotin, where he sometimes lived. After four years, McLean declared Fort Chilcotin "a dead loss" and closed both posts. Having worked for the HBC for over 15 years, the trader probably thought he'd seen it all. He wasn't used to closing up trading posts—and neither was his employer.

It wasn't the fear of attack that prompted the closures. It was lack of business. While Natives continually begged and bartered at Fort Alexandria, employees on the plateau likely never saw a potential customer for weeks at a time. For McLean, a man on the rise in the company, it was undoubtedly a maddening experience.

McLean's disappointment must have fed his bitter contempt for Natives. He had worked with them for years; he had learned their languages. He had likely long shared HBC governor George Simpson's sentiment that "An enlightened Indian is good for nothing." In McLean's view, Indians (any Indians, not just the Tsilhqot'in) couldn't be trusted. He regarded them as "ungrateful, bloodthirsty, treacherous, and cowardly scoundrels." Most HBC men felt the same way. Dealings with Indians were almost always difficult, especially with the Tsilhqot'in, whose haughty, independent attitude had caused McLean's only failure.

But not all Natives suffered the enmity of Kuschte te'kukkpe, or "Fierce Chief," as the Natives called McLean. After all, he had lived with at least three of them. But there were good reasons for that. A man needed all the help he

No white man knew the Tsilhqot'in better than Donald, McLean, the Alexandria expedition's legendary second-in-command.

could get to survive in the wretched wilderness, preferably a hard-working wife who could bear lots of healthy children. Donald McLean had chosen well. By 1862, he had fathered five children and was not done yet. His father, a Red River colonist, and his own trading experience had taught him what white men could expect of Natives. The land and its people taught him more.

Epidemic

After a day or two, the small party of whites resting at Nancootlem decided they could not linger any longer. They mounted up, leaving their ailing companions with the Tsilhqot'in. The reason for their quick departure is not difficult to guess: the two men they left vomiting and shaking inside one of the wooden houses had contracted smallpox.

It is likely the men had become infected at Bella Coola. When Lieutenant Palmer stepped ashore in June to undertake his survey of the Bentinck Arm route, the disease had already reduced the Nuxalk to a fraction of their original number. Little wonder that Palmer and his men ran into trouble. Far from being "willing to do almost anything," as the Bentinck Arm Company's advertisement claimed, the suffering Natives were outraged.

The young son of a Nuxalk chief challenged the lieutenant to a fight. Palmer knocked the man off his feet and threatened to shoot him. It was a bad move. Palmer was forced to carefully negotiate his way out of a tense showdown with 50 desperate, angry Natives.

The disease that had decimated and enraged the coastal peoples was now ready to do its deadly work in the heart of Chilcotin country. A few days after the Cariboo-bound visitors departed, some of the usually energetic villagers at

Nancootlem were smitten with an overwhelming lethargy. Their heads began to pound viciously. A heavy, aching sensation that seemed to radiate from their backs had them wincing with every move they made. Within hours, they were bringing up everything they had eaten. In an attempt to ease the sudden fever that racked their bodies, many stumbled to the lake or nearby creeks and plunged into the cooling waters. Some never emerged. Others crawled out onto the shore, where they collapsed in a delirious, semi-comatose state.

Clutching their charm pouches, the *diyins*, or shamans, sang and gesticulated desperately. Using their age-old method of easing suffering, they laid their hands on the panting, sweating bodies of the afflicted to suck out the illness. Then, cupping their hands close to their faces, they quickly opened them up so the sickness could fly away. But soon, the shamans themselves were silenced. Unvaccinated Caucasians could survive for weeks, spotted with oozing pustules and shaking with repeated fevers, but the Natives' torment was short-lived: most victims died within two days.

Almost overnight, the bodies of dozens of fathers and sons, mothers and daughters lay scattered throughout the village. Little energy remained for the weeping, weakened relatives to carry the dying beneath the aspen and poplar, or to tie thrashing children to the trees to keep them from harming themselves. Few were left who could bury or cremate the dead. Their frightened chief ordered those who could walk or ride to move out—fast. Soon the village was deserted but for the wolves feasting on the dead.

Weeks later, two Bella Coola traders named Angus McLeod and Jim Taylor rode to Nancootlem, hoping to do some trading with smallpox survivors who had returned to the nearly decimated village. In the trees not far away, the two whites discovered many blankets covering the dead. Some of the blankets were nearly new. Covering their mouths and nostrils, the two men quickly gathered up as many of them as they could. Back at the village, they made some trades, no doubt chuckling as the gullible Natives took back the same blankets they had placed around the dead and dying just a few weeks before.

The spread of smallpox on the Chilcotin Plateau through infected blankets was a single for-profit event, quite unlike the formal strategy of biological warfare practised by the British to defeat Ottawa chief Pontiac a century before. Lord Jeffrey Amherst had ordered Colonel Henry Bouquet—who came up with the idea—to "inoculate the Indians by means of blankets." However, this distinction would have meant nothing to the devastated Native peoples of Britain's western colonies.

Terror on the Trail

Puntzi Lake ranch operator William Manning had become frustrated when he noticed Tsilhqot'in tents nestled under the trees by the pretty little spring that watered his partner's pack-train horses. The Tsilhqot'in had used the spring as a convenient stopping point for generations. If Manning knew this, he likely didn't care.

Manning and Alex McDonald had worked tirelessly to make the pack trains and hayfields profitable. He didn't fancy sharing the water with Indians. The effects of the smallpox epidemic were no secret to the angry rancher, and he concocted a strategy to rid himself of these interlopers. In no uncertain terms, he had told Tahpit, chief of the Puntzi Lake Tsilhqot'in, to leave or he would send smallpox into the camp. The next day, the terrified Tsilhqot'in disappeared.

When the word of Manning's threat reached Chief Anahim, the chief's sorrow flared into anger. Another chief, a relative of Anahim, shared that rage. This chief, Klatsassin, was not of hereditary nobility. He was, instead, a war chief. Tall, blue-eyed Klatsassin had gained his power and prestige by conquering the Tsilhqot'in's traditional enemies. He was both revered and feared, and his battle exploits were legendary. But Klatsassin was also a family man, with two wives and six children, and an enemy he was powerless to fight had placed his terrified family in mortal danger. This insidious enemy passed invisibly through stockade walls and invaded their houses, cutting down friends and relatives at every hand. Klatsassin realized this was one battle he could not win, so he and his family fled with the others at Nancootlem, away from the dead and dying.

By early fall, Bentinck Arm packer Robert McLeod,

who had ridden past Nancootlem with his pack train, was also dead. McLeod wasn't a victim of smallpox, but of the people who had been ravaged by it. As he led his horses near McDonald and Manning's Puntzi Lake ranch, some Tsilhqot'in were waiting in the trailside brush. The ambush was swift and terrifying. As horses plunged and whinnied and men screamed, McLeod was quickly cut down.

Enterprising Jim Taylor and Angus McLeod had done good business with the Tsilhqot'in up and down the trail. The blankets they had salvaged at Nancootlem were snapped up, just as they knew they would be. But a few days later, Angus McLeod could not rouse himself from his own blankets. Taylor looked on uneasily as his feverish partner twitched and moaned. Taylor had been immunized against smallpox, but McLeod hadn't been. Soon, McLeod was dead.

Not long after, the Tsilhqot'in began to sicken and die once again. Smallpox raced across the Fraser River and struck the Natives of the Cariboo. By the winter of 1863, sections of the gold-seekers' trail were lined with tents housing pox victims waiting for death. No graves could be dug in the frozen ground, so the hundreds who had already succumbed would lie under hummocks of snow until spring.

Many kilometres to the west, in the land of the Tsilhqot'in, the disease had finally burned itself out. The once proud, prosperous people of Chief Anahim, his rival Chief Alexis and their war chief, Klatsassin, had numbered 1,500. Now there were fewer than 800 dispirited, starving souls.

5

Roadwork

AS ANOTHER DISMAL VICTORIA WINTER wore on, Alfred Waddington had time to soberly reflect upon the hardships his crew had endured at the inlet. He must have feared what they would face in the coming spring. The company's one-year charter was too short to complete the road, let alone provide profits from freight tolls. Obtaining a charter extension was an absolute necessity. In late January 1863, Waddington wrote to mainland government officials. Deciding to play it safe, he wrote, "Ten years would be none too long," and offered to lower tolls from five cents to three cents a ton.

Surprise Visitors on the Inlet

Waddington and his work gang were not the only visitors

to Bute Inlet that year. During the winter, when Alex McDonald had ventured down the Homathko Canyon to the sea, he found that others had already travelled to Bute Inlet. Near the head of the inlet, McDonald encountered dozens of Tsilhqot'in. He was shocked. When the Tsilhqot'in made their way into the upper reaches of Homalco territory, they did so for a brief period in the summer fishing season. Yet, here they were in the middle of winter, in the midst of the Homalco, Euclataw and Klahoose peoples on the inlet.

When Waddington later saw the Native riverside camp of about 250 just above the inlet, he shared McDonald's surprise. Where had they come from, and why were they there? Waddington found the presence of the Tsilhqot'in, under the leadership of a minor chief named Telloot, even more startling. The summer before, when half a dozen Tsilhqot'in come down to trade saw the coastal Euclataws there, scooping up the small, oil-rich eulachon, the interior Natives had fled back upriver.

There was a compelling reason for this new spirit of relatively peaceful co-existence. Beset by smallpox and a scarcity of food on the plateau, the Tsilhqot'in had been close to starving. They had moved to the inlet in a desperate search for food. They had also heard about the road project. Perhaps the white men would put them to work and feed them. The Tsilhqot'in and the others had waited out the winter for the arrival of those they called "King George Men."

As he sailed up past the inlet mouth on board a steamer

aptly named *Enterprise*, Waddington was troubled to see that the Native camp was located on the site of his future town. Their choice of the broad and relatively flat site made sense; nevertheless, they would have to be moved. Waddington decided to seek out Telloot, and when he found him, surprise followed surprise.

The chief spoke some English and carried around a fragment of an 1847 edition of the *Illustrated London News*. In the newspaper's margin was a scribble from Captain Thomas Price, an early Bute explorer and Royal Engineer: "Telloot, Chilcoaten [sic] chief, a good guide—faithful and trustworthy." In his long business career, Waddington had read dozens of letters of reference, but none like this one. The bargaining began and presents were offered. Telloot went to work, and within 24 hours the townsite was cleared.

While helping unload the steamer that weekend, the Natives got an unpleasant surprise. The visitors had brought 19 mules and horses with them, which meant there would be few packing jobs that season. Waddington was bemused at the dismay of the devastated Natives. "All awaited their prey like vultures," Waddington wrote De Cosmos in a letter published in the *British Colonist* that summer. The Natives "were not a little disappointed when they saw the mules landed."

Keeping the Peace

Not long after *Enterprise* sailed away, Waddington and others heard screams and shouts echoing from another camp nearby. When they investigated, Waddington found "a number of our Indians were raving mad with drink." Two years before, Waddington had successfully outlawed liquor sales to Victoria Natives. He was now determined to stop any liquor traffic that might imperil his progress up the inlet. Both his scheme's success and his men's safety depended upon swift action. His target was not the imbibing Homalco, but unscrupulous traders.

For Waddington, the incident at the mouth of the Homathko River represented more than a menace. It was an opportunity. Decisive action against the traders would make him a hero with the Natives. He and 10 others jumped into a large canoe and paddled down the inlet. It took less than half an hour to locate one of the two traders. On his boat was a 10-gallon keg holding the remains of a mind-destroying concoction of—among other stomach-churning ingredients— nitric acid, chewing tobacco, ink and pepper. Drinking copious quantities of the vile liquid often resulted in madness and death and could lead to bloody retribution. Waddington's men dumped the contents of the merchant's keg into the inlet and told him to take his trade elsewhere or forfeit his boat. The trader rowed away, threatening lawsuits.

Down near the mouth of the inlet, town lots were being surveyed. The monotonous thud of a piledriver signalled the construction of a wharf that extended into what was now called Waddington Harbour, and a store was being hammered together out of boards brought up expressly for the purpose. On the trail, choppers and bridgers were hard at work. Much to Waddington's dismay, at least 10 of the bridges built the previous season had washed away in spring flooding. Progress slowed while repairs were made.

Taking the easiest route up toward the canyon meant the Homathko River had to be crossed. Men began to construct a large scow, which would be guided across the swift-flowing river by rope pulley, and chopped down trees to build a combination storehouse and home for the ferry operator, former British soldier Tim Smith.

It soon became obvious that the mules were useless in the rough terrain. If the Tsilhqot'in wanted to pack, let them pack, Waddington decided. Besides, their knowledge of the upper country could be helpful. This new arrangement would bring them into close contact with crew members, so Waddington gave orders that the Natives and their families were not to be interfered with. Mess with these people, he warned his men, and you'll be shipped back to Victoria on the first available steamer. It quickly became apparent that keeping the peace wasn't going to be that easy.

Muskets, but No Food
In addition to being paid for their work, the Tsilhqot'in expected to be fed. Foreman William Brewster decided otherwise. Brewster was quite willing to pay Telloot and his followers with cooking utensils, blankets, clothing and even muskets, powder and shot, but he refused them food.

It was hard to ignore hungry little children, though. Workmen surreptitiously handed campfire tidbits to Tsilhqot'in youngsters. Telloot's son-in-law, a young Tsilhqot'in worker named Chedekki, watched Brewster snatch morsels of food out of the children's hands and throw them into the campfire. Tension began to mount.

When four Tsilhqot'in packers farther up the trail were offered a little breakfast before hoisting their 75-pound packs, they naturally made the most of the opportunity. Hour after hour, they gorged themselves on bacon, beans, rice, dried apples, sugar and bread covered in molasses. Later, they lounged around the campsite, puffing on their slate pipes. When others suggested it was time they hit the trail with their heavy loads, they merely laughed. Commissary Frederick Saunders was incensed. He thought the Tsilhqot'in "a dirty, thriftless lot" requiring "no small degree of scheming tact in the management of them."

Soon after, Telloot and nearly a dozen followers wandered into the road crew's canyon camp. Cunning Telloot engaged Saunders in conversation while his men darted in and out of workers' tents, grabbing anything they could "with much laughter and derision." Saunders knew what was happening, but, because he was alone, the commissary did nothing. Later, however, he complained to surveyor Henry McNeill.

McNeill was a veteran wilderness explorer who had survived Homfray's horrific Bute expedition. Not one to employ "scheming tact," he took Telloot aside to tell him exactly what he thought of his behaviour and that of his tribesmen. As a tough-looking, disfigured Tsilhqot'in called Scarface sauntered by, McNeill spotted two workers' knives inside his quiver. The surveyor flung his leg out, sending the thief sprawling into the campfire. As Scarface rolled about in pain, the knives and a large cut of tobacco spilled onto the ground. McNeill and Telloot forced Scarface to point out the other thieves. After he had done so, McNeill repossessed the articles and sternly ordered Telloot and his followers out of the camp.

At the ferry crossing, a group of Tsilhqot'in brazenly asked Tim Smith for food. Smith refused. Far from being intimidated, one man pulled a knife. Within seconds, burly Smith pinned him to the ground and snatched away his blade. As the Tsilhqot'in left, Smith might have congratulated himself on his victory. However, he had made a grave mistake. He had bested a Tsilhqot'in warrior—but then allowed him to live.

If they couldn't get free food from Brewster or Smith, the Tsilhqot'in were compelled to find it elsewhere. After blankets, muskets and ammunition were distributed in payment for their work, the Tsilhqot'in disappeared up the trail to fish for trout at Tatla Lake, on the other side of the mountains. By late August, the salmon were running on the Homathko. Telloot and a few others came back down to the upper reaches of the river, and the chief was still loitering around the trail camps in early September.

Trustworthy Natives

Unlike the other Tsilhqot'in, Telloot and Chedekki, whom the whites called "George," enjoyed a special status with white visitors. Chedekki was quiet and helpful, and he profited by his acquiescent behaviour. He and his wife, Telloot's daughter, received food while the others went hungry, although cautious workers insisted the couple eat inside a cabin, out of sight of the others. In her husband's absence, Telloot's wife and their children were also given food.

By September, Waddington had hired Telloot as his guide on a trek up the trail through the mountains to the Chilcotin country. Perhaps Captain Price's reference had something to do with his decision about hiring the "good guide." Waddington may also have seen the wisdom of getting the chief away from Brewster and the road crew.

Dynamite and Detour

Climbing through the Homathko Canyon, Waddington saw for himself the breathtaking grandeur that later inspired a CPR surveyor to rhapsodize over "towering rocks thousands of feet high . . . a mountain torrent—whirling, boiling, roaring, over huge boulders." Was *this* what Tiedeman had encountered? The surveyor had mentioned "bluffs," but nothing in his report had prepared Waddington's road crews for these enormous walls of sheer rock.

Large drills were used to hammer out holes for dynamite charges. The blasts were impressively loud, but attempts to gouge out a gallery big enough for a roadbed through perpendicular canyon walls were slow and expensive. Waddington called a halt. It was not impossible to build the road this way, he argued, simply too costly. A detour was proposed. Discouraged crewmen abandoned all they had accomplished—as little as that was—and considered a different route.

A small group of men under the guidance of a William Manning ranch hand had set out to explore alternatives. Not only did they fail to find a route, the attempt almost cost them their lives. The ranch hand got the explorers hopelessly lost and then took their only gun, abandoning them to their fate. When they emerged three weeks later, they were close to starvation.

In mid-September, as Waddington walked out onto the Chilcotin grasslands, Brewster arrived in Victoria to recruit more workers. The road will be through the mountains before the end of the fall, the foreman told reporters. Many remained skeptical. On the other side of the strait, John Robson began ratcheting up the anti-Bute rhetoric again.

A month later, Waddington was back in Victoria. Yes, he conceded, the activity through the canyon was "very expensive" work. Furthermore, he admitted, while the trail was not entirely open at this point, it would be open in the spring.

Most of the workers left the inlet early in December, but Brewster and 20 cold and lonely workmen remained, still clawing a roadbed through the Homathko Canyon, trying to make good on the foreman's prediction.

CHAPTER

6

An Act of War

THE BUTE INLET WAGON ROAD COMPANY was mired in debt. Sick and exhausted, William Brewster returned to Victoria later that winter and discovered there was no pay for him. Suppliers' bills remained outstanding, and more capital was needed for the company's "final" work season the next spring. Worse, 700 of the 1,200 company shares offered to the public the year before still remained unsold.

Not surprisingly, support for the Bute Inlet road had dwindled. Overly optimistic Waddington had consistently underestimated and publicly understated the formidable natural barriers that delayed the road's completion. Slow progress and unguarded negative comments from disenchanted workers further fuelled public skepticism.

Meanwhile, the pace of work on the Cariboo Road was accelerating. At the north end of the Fraser Canyon, one contractor had even spanned the river with a 90-metre suspension bridge. The cost was $45,000—almost as much as the Bute company's entire expenditures to date.

Bute Inlet Road Company directors were disheartened and decided to cut their losses. An extraordinary meeting was called to wind up the company. By the end of the meeting, the directors and chairman had agreed to auction it off. That way, at least the directors would recoup some of their investments.

His directors may not have possessed the tenacity and courage needed to overcome adversity, but Waddington did. He would demonstrate that at the company auction. But first he had to have an auction of his own. It was time to put his money where his mouth was.

In January 1864, Waddington decided to liquidate dozens of lots and the businesses situated on them, including the Albion Saloon. The sale brought Waddington almost $39,000. Considering he had paid as little as $100 a lot for the raw land around Fort Victoria years before, Waddington should have been pleased, but there would have been little pleasure in taking such drastic action out of desperation.

On April 14, the Bute Inlet Wagon Road Company was offered for sale. "Contrary to expectation," the *British Colonist* reported, "there was considerable bidding." The final bid of $14,000—"considered rather cheap," the newspaper noted— was made by the firm's former chairman. Alfred Waddington walked away from the auction the sole owner of the debt-ridden company. The rest of the proceeds from his property sale would soon disappear, sucked into the increasingly costly project as surely as if he had tossed the heavy gold coins into the foaming waters of the Homathko River.

The Theft

At the end of March 1864, John Clark and the few others now living year round at the Bute Inlet townsite watched William Brewster and his men disembark from the chartered schooner. The settlers were relieved. Living amongst the nearly starving Homalco, Euclataw, Klahoose and Tsilhqot'in had been dangerous. Natives had threatened Clark himself a number of times.

Among those who heard Clark's tales was Frederick Whymper. Waddington had hired the noted British illustrator to capture the awe-inspiring scenery in paintings designed to fire the imagination of potential investors in England. Everything the impressionable artist saw around the village and up the trail seemed to bear out what others said about the Tsilhqot'in. It appeared they preferred "half-starving in winter to exerting themselves," he later told the *British Colonist*. Whymper watched them fight with their dogs for "anything that we threw out of our camp ... bones, bacon-rind or tea-leaves."

Why hunt for scarce game, the Natives likely reasoned, when there was food sitting on the shelves inside the townsite storehouse? Brewster learned the worst: during the winter, the storehouse had been broken into and every one of the 25 large sacks of flour carried off. Brewster was determined to bring the guilty parties to justice. He started by questioning Chedekki. Brewster could have interrogated Chessus, whom he had hired to safeguard the storehouse, but he likely suspected that Chessus was the thief. Friendly, trustworthy Chedekki thought Brewster was accusing him.

"You know I've have been with you three years and have never stolen anything from you," Chedekki argued.

"No," Brewster agreed impatiently, "but I want to find out who *did* take it."

Chedekki either couldn't or wouldn't say who had taken the critical food supply. Brewster gave up and put him to work loading the heavy drilling equipment onto the mules.

A Deadly Threat

A few weeks later, a number of Tsilhqot'in families walked up the trail to ask for work. Here was Brewster's opportunity. Before he was going to give any of them work, the angry foreman told them, he had to know who had stolen the flour. When his information-for-work gambit got no response, he decided on another strategy. He would hire them, but they wouldn't be paid until they had worked out the value of the missing flour. The Tsilhqot'in bristled.

"You are in our country," one spoke out. "You owe us bread." Although he used the word "bread," he likely meant its main ingredient: flour. It was an interesting statement. Now at work near the third bluff above the ferry, the crew had, indeed, entered traditional Tsilhqot'in territory. But if he was aware of that, Brewster gave no indication that he cared. *Owe us*? The contemptuous demand was enough to set Brewster's blood boiling.

The foreman reached for a notebook and dug into his pocket for a stub of pencil. He asked a translator to give him the name of every Tsilhqot'in standing around them. When his list was complete, Brewster told the translator to explain to them what he had done.

The Tsilhqot'in grew agitated. Writing was an alien act they barely understood. To write down a man's name appeared to be the same as stealing it. Standing nearby, Chedekki watched as his concerned tribesmen murmured amongst themselves. Why, they asked, had Brewster stolen their names? The translator relayed the question.

"I have taken down your names because you haven't told me who has stolen the flour," Brewster replied. Yes, he wanted to get to get to the bottom of this theft, but now there was something more at stake: control. Brewster decided that he needed to use fear to keep these Tsilhqot'in in their place.

He turned to his translator. "Tell them," he yelled, "All the Chilcotins are going to *die*! The whites'll introduce sickness into the country which will kill you all!"

A few days later, satisfied that the Natives now understood who held the power of life and death, Brewster magnanimously decided to hire many of them, including Telloot. The foreman might not have noticed that the taciturn youth named Piell had left the camp immediately after the confrontation. If the foreman had noticed him at all, he likely gave no thought to his quiet disappearance. The Tsilhqot'in were coming and going all the time.

Brewster had no way of knowing that Piell was on his way downriver to the townsite to tell his father of the foreman's fearsome threat of disease and death. It might have given Brewster pause had he known that Piell was the eldest son of the Tsilhqot'in war chief named Klatsassin.

The Final Frustration

Klatsassin had come to the head of the inlet with his family weeks before. It wasn't work or even food that brought the war chief. He had come to rescue his daughter, whom the Euclataws had kidnapped. Stealing another tribe's women, children and even young men was an age-old tradition among BC's Aboriginal peoples. In this risky game of inter-tribal one-upmanship, absconding with a war chief's daughter was a daring and potentially profitable feat.

Klatsassin knew he had to be cautious. The Tsilhqot'in were barely tolerated in Coast Salish territory. The Euclataws and their allies, the Homalco, greatly outnumbered his people. Engaging in open warfare with those who held his daughter near where Tsilhqot'in women and children were living would be inviting disaster. Moreover, the white men wouldn't tolerate any violence that hindered their work. Attacking the Euclataws was not an option.

Klatsassin decided to ask Alfred Waddington to negotiate the return of his daughter. This was not as farfetched as it might have seemed. Two autumns before, Waddington had successfully bartered for a coastal chief's daughter who had been kidnapped by a rival tribe. It helped that Waddington spoke Chinook Jargon. Klatsassin had a hunch that the Euclataws, as eager for work and food as the Tsilhqot'in, would heed the wishes of the white chief. For that reason, Klatsassin hoped that he would regain his daughter at little or no cost. All it had taken for Waddington to rescue the previous captive was a mere 16 blankets.

Klatsassin was disappointed to find that Waddington was not among the workers when they stepped off their boat. No one seemed certain when he would appear. Frustrated, Klatsassin sent his teenaged son Piell up the trail to ask if anyone in the canyon knew when Waddington would arrive. However, the frightened boy had brought back news that had nothing to do with Waddington. Instead, he delivered an account that horrified and incensed his father. Brewster had threatened them all with deadly smallpox.

All the terror he had seen, all the sorrow he had felt during the recent epidemic must have come back to the angry war chief in a rush. There seemed to be no difference between the threat made by Manning at Puntzi Lake and the one made by Brewster. Neither Anahim nor Tahpit had done anything to stop Manning. No one knew how the whites managed to spread this horrible death, but the settler's threat had become a terrible reality; the sickness had been visited upon Klatsassin's people a second time.

The time for diplomacy with the Euclataws was over. There was a far greater issue at stake. Klatsassin humbled himself before the rival chief and began negotiations for his daughter. The Euclataw drove a hard bargain. Klatsassin swallowed his pride and bartered away a canoe, six blankets and a musket for his daughter's return. Putting his humiliation behind him, the Tsilhqot'in war chief quickly gathered up his wives and children and left Waddington's townsite, accompanied by Cushen and Scarface.

Klatsassin had originally planned to quietly wind his way back through the mountains via the Memeya River. Instead, he and the others headed for the Homathko Canyon. Up the trail, past the ferry, he would hold a council with Telloot and other Tsilhqot'in regarding Brewster and the danger the whites' presence represented. In the war chief's mind, Brewster's threat was an act of war.

When the Tsilhqot'in declared war, tradition decreed that hereditary chiefs—Telloot, Anahim, and even Anahim's most powerful rival, the mighty Alexis—bow before Klatsassin. This *was* war, Klatsassin decided, and he would lead his people into battle as he had many times before. Only now, he would not lead them against the Shuswap, Carriers or Homalco. This time, the Tsilhqot'in would battle the whites.

7

War's Drumbeat

EVEN BEFORE ALFRED WADDINGTON HAD been forced to buy out his directors, a more grandiose vision than a mere wagon road had taken shape in the mind of the obsessive entrepreneur. As far back as 1858, Amor De Cosmos had written about the possibility of a railroad to the Pacific coast. Waddington was now convinced that the ultimate purpose of his wagon road was to be a roadbed for rails. The Bute Inlet town of Waddington would boast a waterfront train station. Tracks would run down the middle of the wharf, and trains would be shunted onto large barges for the short overnight trip to Victoria. Waddington had resolved to keep the company alive and was determined that nothing would stand in the way of the destiny of British Columbia's future transportation titan.

In New Westminster's *Columbian*, John Robson sneered at the plight of "Poor Old Waddy." The impoverished road builder, Robson warned, was "beginning to reap the natural fruits of his persistent and consummate folly." No one could have predicted how bitter those fruits would prove to be.

Death at the Ferry

Up the Homathko River, artist Frederick Whymper had been busy. Guided by Telloot, Whymper had been tramping up and down the trail, anxious to find scenic subjects for his sketchbook. Finally, he was led to the foot of the formidable Tiedeman Glacier. He sketched the impressive scene and returned to William Brewster's advance camp. Packing with him Brewster's latest report to Waddington in Victoria, Whymper proceeded down the trail, sketching as he went. At the ferry, Whymper stayed overnight with Tim Smith and joined a pack train the next morning for the return trip to the townsite. He didn't stay with the group for long. Once he caught sight of Waddington Glacier, he was off again into the bush to capture the majestic scene.

But Whymper wasn't the only visitor to call on Tim Smith that week. On Thursday morning, April 28, Klatsassin, his family and companions reached the river crossing and were joined by two others, Chessus and Yahooslas. As he sent the ferry over, Smith watched the group carefully from the opposite bank. The ferryman had an idea what they wanted—and it wasn't simply ferry transport.

Once off the scow, Cushen and Scarface wandered up the trail. And sure enough, Klatsassin walked right up to Smith, and demanded food and blankets. In Smith's mind, the war chief was just another Indian beggar. The former Royal Engineer sapper had no time for beggars—especially armed ones like these—and made it plain that he would give them nothing. Orders were orders, and Brewster had it right. No food, not even for work. To Smith, these people didn't look too eager for work, and what began as unsuccessful begging might become stealing. Yahooslas was a known thief, and where was Chessus when the flour was stolen?

Before Smith realized what was happening, Klatsassin stepped inside the storehouse. With a startled cry, Smith followed him in. When Klatsassin turned around, he had folded blankets in his hands. Smith blocked his way and snatched at the blankets. There was a brief scuffle, each man pulling the blankets this way and that way. Smith managed to wrench the blankets from the war chief's hands. He ordered him outside and told them all to move up the trail.

Klatsassin and his group did not move very far. That evening, they watched Smith at his campfire, cooking the food that they had been denied. Chessus and Yahooslas began murmuring incessantly to the chief, urging him to make the white man pay for his arrogance and insults. Already in an ugly mood, Klatsassin did not need much convincing.

Unaware he was being observed, Smith finished his supper, then leaned against a large tree and lit up his pipe.

Klatsassin carefully sighted down the barrel of his musket at the stationary target across the clearing. This was easy. He pulled the trigger. As the report of the gun echoed down the river, Smith's head bounced against the tree. The breeze wafted the gunsmoke away, and the warriors watched the ferryman collapse heavily to the ground, blood running from the small round hole in his forehead.

Klatsassin threw down his musket and ran to the fallen man. Smith's arms were flung back, buttons and belt wrenched free, and all three warriors pulled shirt, boots and pants from Smith's body. Then, the Tsilhqot'in dragged the stripped victim to the water's edge and kicked him into the swiftly flowing river.

Pulling on Smith's red-striped shirt, Klatsassin dashed into the storehouse, his two companions close behind. They had gone without for long enough. Tonight, the men and their wives and children would feast. Tomorrow, they would continue to avenge themselves on these threatening intruders.

Gathering His Forces

Farther up the trail, William Brewster told Telloot to go down to the ferry and haul up more provisions for the men in the camp. He gave Telloot a note instructing the ferryman to pay the chief a blanket for the work. Telloot told Chedekki that he was leaving with a friendly Homalco called Squinteye and that they would be back that night.

As they crested a small hill above the ferry, Telloot

and Squinteye were surprised to meet Klatsassin and his group. Telloot told the others that he and Squinteye were going down to pick up supplies at the ferry. Klatsassin casually indicated that they needn't go any farther. Amused at Telloot's confusion, Chessus couldn't keep quiet. "Our chief has killed the white man at the ferry!" he blurted.

A disbelieving Telloot looked about for confirmation. Klatsassin and Piell nodded. It was true. Telloot erupted angrily. What had hotheaded Klatsassin done? He threatened to hurry back up the trail to tell Brewster.

It was an awkward moment for Klatsassin. He had intended to build support at the Tsilhqot'in camp that night and didn't need another chief putting the enemy on guard and undermining his plans. Before Klatsassin could respond, Squinteye spoke up, "Why did you Tsilhqot'in do it?" Like most coastal people, Squinteye's Homalco enjoyed a good relationship with the whites. A killing put them all in jeopardy. The whites likely wouldn't discriminate between Tsilhqot'in and Homalco.

Klatsassin needed to show deference to Telloot, a fellow Tsilhqot'in chief, but not to a lowly Homalco. The war chief wrenched Squinteye's musket out of his hand and handed it to Chessus. "Keep quiet or you'll end up like the ferryman," Klatsassin warned. Telloot listened closely. Squinteye was of no further use to Klatsassin; the war chief needed to get rid of him quickly. Klatsassin told the Homalco he was free to go down to the townsite, but to tell no one what

The Homathko Canyon, *circa* 1875, and a fragment of Waddington's "road." To support the wooden roadbed, poles were wedged into holes drilled into the sheer cliff.

he had learned. To encourage Squinteye's silence, Klatsassin rewarded him with two blankets from the trashed ferry storehouse and sent him on his way.

Even though the Homalco would probably side with the whites, Klatsassin likely didn't much care if Squinteye told anyone. He wouldn't reach the townsite until the next day, and even if the whites believed him, they would huddle in their cabins for another day or two, deciding what to do—if anything—before organizing themselves to do it.

And Telloot's threat to tell Brewster? Wait until I speak with Cushen, Scarface and others at the camp, Klatsassin suggested to the old chief. Then, if you still want to, you can say whatever you like. While Telloot hesitated, Klatsassin told him about Brewster's deadly smallpox threat.

That evening around the fire, Klatsassin spoke before 12 tribesmen at their camp, less than 100 metres from the workers' tents. He had no fear that his words would provoke the whites, simply because none of them understood what he was saying. The suppressed fury of Klatsassin's tense monologue galvanized his listeners.

The whites were invaders in Tsilhqot'in country, Klatsassin told them. They behaved as if they owned it. Had there been any discussion of compensation? Never. Instead, these men hunted and fished, taking food out of the mouths of the Tsilhqot'in people, and refused to share their own supplies. What made it even worse was that these men mistreated them, especially the women. It was no secret that hungry women bartered for food for themselves and their children, with nothing to trade but their own bodies. Worst of all was the white sickness that had decimated their people. Now Brewster had threatened to bring more of it.

Klatsassin fell silent and his listeners murmured amongst themselves. Everything Klatsassin said felt right and true. So what was their war chief suggesting? It was simple. All the whites must die. Only then would the country be free of them and the people be safe. Before his followers could debate the feasibility of killing every white man on the trail, Klatsassin put their minds at ease. Did the whites have guns? No. They had traded them all away. All but four of the Tsilhqot'in around the fire had muskets and ammunition. The rest had knives and heavy hatchets.

Earlier that day, Brewster and three others had gone farther up the trail, leaving Charles Buttle, the cook, in charge. That left just 12 men in the camp—no match for the armed warriors. Besides, in the traditional manner of the Tsilhqot'in, the enemy would be given no hint of what was to come. There likely would be no resistance at all. The time was right.

And after? Think of the food, the blankets, the clothes and other goods they would carry away over the mountains to the Tsilhqot'in people at Chilko Lake and to others at Puntzi and Anahim lakes. Klatsassin looked about as Telloot sat in silence. It was settled.

The round, hand-held drum came out. The pounding rhythm began. In ones and twos, the men got to their feet and, gesturing and whooping, began to pivot and whirl before the fire. Near the tents, graceful silhouettes began to sway. The women, too, had caught the magic. Wide-eyed children stared out from behind tent flaps. The insistent tempo of the drum accented the shouted recitation of brave deeds, great conquests, past glories and the battle to come.

An Uneasy Night

That night, Charles Buttle suggested everyone turn in early.

Most, including George Smith and Alex Millan, needed no invitation. Like fellow crewmen Robert Pollock and John Hoffman, they were tired and eager to crawl into their white canvas tents. Pete Petersen, Joe Newman and James Campbell bade each other goodnight.

From time to time, Ed Mosley, Phil Buckley and some others had glanced in the direction of the Native camp. They hadn't seen the Tsilhqot'in dance like this before. And when some of them came over to talk, their faces were smeared with a different kind of paint than usual. What did that mean? Nobody really understood these people.

It's unlikely anyone gave much thought to how well they would sleep, even with all the singing and drumming nearby. After another long day of exhausting physical labour, Jimmy Openshaw, tentmate John Newman and most of the rest were bone-weary and probably felt they could sleep through anything. Besides, who would be fool enough to go over and demand that the Tsilhqot'in stop their racket?

As he turned in with the rest of them, Chedekki likely felt lonely. Not only had his wife and children left the day before with others returning to the lakes on the plateau, it did not appear that Telloot would be joining him and the whites in sleep. Chedekki was almost certainly feeling uneasy. He had noticed a number of things that the whites had not, including the fact that Telloot was back in camp. Chedekki had expected to see the chief and Squinteye drop off supplies to Buttle in the whites' camp and then join them for supper.

Instead, Telloot had gone straight to the Tsilhqot'in's fire. And for someone who had walked all the way to the ferry and back, Telloot had returned earlier than expected. But where were the supplies? And where was Squinteye?

It was fortunate for Telloot that Brewster was away from the camp. With no additional supplies for Buttle's cookfire, the foreman would have demanded answers from Chedekki's father-in-law. At this moment, Chedekki had no idea of how unfortunate Brewster's absence would be for everyone in the two camps. Had the foreman questioned Telloot as McNeill had questioned him a year before about the thefts, the next 24 hours might have unfolded very differently.

Another thing probably puzzled Chedekki: why had Klatsassin, Chessus and Yahooslas come up the trail? Perhaps they were just on their way back home, but maybe not. All these puzzles might be solved in the morning after Chedekki talked with Telloot. Then, the chief could explain something that must have worried Chedekki the most: the insistent, throbbing drum and the high-pitched wail of the song he and the others were hearing. This was no song of celebration. It was something else, and that almost-certain knowledge—and the fact that he was employed and fed by the whites—were probably the reasons why Chedekki was unwilling to join his tribesmen.

As night fell, the main camp of the Bute Inlet Road Company's crew was dark and quiet. Not far away, voices rose in their wailing song against the thump of the drum.

8

Canyon Slaughter

ON THE NIGHT OF APRIL 29, Frederick Whymper and four workmen ate an early supper in a large Native lodge that sometimes provided accommodation for packers and road-crew members at the Waddington townsite. It had been a satisfying trip for the artist, but a long and tiring one that wasn't over yet. The next day, he and two others would begin the potentially dangerous canoe voyage down the strait to Vancouver Island. Almost as soon as their meal was finished, Whymper and the others turned in.

At 3 a.m., Squinteye and a number of excited Homalcos barged in. When they got the Natives calmed down enough to be coherent, the five men heard that Tim Smith had been killed. The whites glanced at each other and began to laugh. It wasn't the first rumour of a Native attack. One had surfaced in Victoria the previous spring and been the talk of the town. Supposedly, five crewmen had been slain. A week later, a letter from Waddington had laid the story to rest.

Squinteye told them more. One of the killers was wearing Smith's red-striped shirt. The scow had been set adrift, and flour, blankets and other things had been taken from the storehouse. The whites stopped laughing now. These details gave the far-fetched story the ring of truth.

However, some things still didn't add up. Why would Brewster send *Indians* down with word of a murder? That provoked more ominous questions. What if Smith wasn't the only one killed? Did the crewmen have guns? They wouldn't have many, Whymper guessed. Should someone go up the trail to investigate? In spite of the group's skepticism, nobody thought that was prudent.

Instead, Whymper and the others agreed to delay their departure until noon the next day. If the story had any credence, surely by then they would hear something more. As the men returned to their blankets, Whymper vowed to tell Alfred Waddington to take some weapons the next time he returned to Bute Inlet.

The Ultimatum
Chedekki awoke from his uneasy sleep. Telloot was still not beside him. It was dark, too early to get up, so he rolled over

and closed his eyes again. He awoke again; his leg was being nudged. A familiar silhouette loomed over him.

"Why do you sleep so long?" Telloot asked. "Get up, for Klatsassin wants you."

Chedekki wrapped himself in a blanket and grabbed his musket. He likely had no idea why the war chief wanted to talk with him, but he must have suspected trouble. Perhaps that was why he decided to take his musket along.

The Tsilhqot'in were clustered silently around their dying fire when Chedekki and Telloot arrived. A hand lifted Chedekki's gun from his unresisting hand.

"Sit down with me," Klatsassin commanded, and he motioned Chedekki to follow him. "You have a good heart toward the whites?" Klatsassin asked when they were alone.

"Yes," Chedekki admitted. "They have given me money and food these three years." You didn't lie to a war chief.

"Will you help us?" Klatsassin asked unexpectedly.

Chedekki was puzzled.

"I am going to kill all the whites," Klatsassin continued. "You know they have our names in a book to do that to us."

So, others had told Klatsassin about Brewster's notebook and about his threat of sickness.

"If you do not want to come in with us," Klatsassin said, "give me your gun."

That meant that the gun already taken from him might not be returned. Chedekki would be defenceless, just like the white men in their tents. Then Klatsassin told him, "If you will not go with us, remain with the whites. We will serve you the same." No ultimatum could have been any clearer.

This was a chance to escape death, something the Tsilhqot'in would not offer the white men with whom Chedekki was so closely associated. He might have given a moment's thought to those he worked with: Pete, Ed, Jimmy, Phil and all the rest. Whether he liked them or not didn't matter. In the Tsilhqot'in world, killing any white man in retribution for insults or injury was the same as killing the specific individual—Brewster or Manning—who had wronged them.

Chedekki knew the whites were doomed. "I will go with you," he murmured to the war chief. Klatsassin got up, and Chedekki followed him over to the others. The chief nodded and someone handed the young packer his musket.

Death at First Light

At the main work camp on the bank of the Homathko River, Charles Buttle staggered out of his tent to greet the dawn. Buttle had barely begun to tend to the fire when the quiet of the early morning was shattered by a blood-curdling shriek from the nearby underbrush. The cook fell with two musket balls in his back. The Tsilhqot'in attack had begun.

As Buttle flopped lifeless to the ground amongst the pots and firewood, Klatsassin and his dozen warriors dashed toward the tents, shooting and slashing through the light canvas. A pair of musket balls penetrated deep into John Newman's groin. Another ball shattered Jimmy Openshaw's skull. They were the first to die. Within seconds, Alex Millan and George Smith in the neighbouring tent had breathed their last, two more victims of the first deadly volley of gunfire.

Tsilhqot'in women and children clustered beneath the trees to watch the men at their grisly work. Knives flashed, severing the ropes that held the tents taut above the sleeping men. Canvas billowed and collapsed, clearly outlining the motionless shapes inside. Rifle butts and hatchets swung down on the shrouded, defenceless forms.

A painful glancing blow to the forehead awoke Phil Buckley. Instinctively, he rolled clear of his collapsing tent and jumped to his feet, just inches from Telloot's screaming face. Buckley toppled the Tsilhqot'in chief to the ground, but two others attacked him, their knives arcing through the air and burying themselves in his groin. Buckley took another slash on his left wrist and fell to his knees.

Awakened by the shots that had felled Buttle, Pete Petersen crawled from his blankets and into the murderous melee outside. The butt of a musket cut the air close to his head. Petersen looked up into a familiar face. *Chedekki?*

Out of the corner of his eye, Petersen saw another moustached Tsilhqot'in racing toward him with both hands raised above his head. He jerked away as Chessus buried the head of a hatchet into the ground where he had stood a moment before. Before Chessus could extract his weapon, Petersen stumbled to the riverbank, leaving Robert Pollock behind in the tent, his life bleeding away.

As Buckley collapsed to the ground, Ed Mosley lay in his tent a few feet away, wedged between Joseph Fielding and James Campbell. The entrance flap was flung aside, then two gun barrels exploded at almost point-blank range. The shots hit Fielding and Campbell, but, miraculously, missed the half-hidden Mosley. A moment later, the tent's ridgepole fell across Mosley's torso, trapping him between his writhing companions. Gasping in the acrid gunsmoke, Mosley watched as intruding arms plunged knives deep into the bodies that lay just inches from his own.

Sensing Buckley was finished, his two attackers turned back to his tent. Straddling the fallen canvas, they began to hack John Hoffman to death. Buckley seized this slim chance at survival, hauling himself painfully across the clearing and into the underbrush.

Peering furtively from behind a large tree at the riverbank, Pete Petersen watched Chedekki, musket at the ready, cautiously draw nearer. Chedekki took quick aim and fired. Petersen winced as the ball entered his left arm and sped out through his wrist. Driven wild with pain, Petersen whirled away and threw himself into the river.

Scarcely breathing lest the rise and fall of the suffocating canvas give him away, Ed Mosley lay motionless between his companions' bleeding bodies. The knives had disappeared from the gaping holes they had left. He could still hear whoops and gunfire some distance away. Now, he had to make the most important decision of his life. He could make

82

Sasquatch Gifts & Souvenirs

Tel: 604-446-1880
101-196 Esplanade Ave.
Harrison Hot Springs, BC
GST# 820469187

Location: SASQUATCH
Terminal: 01
Cashier: MILLIE
12/7/2019   3:11:34 PM
Invoice#:   SASQ1912071511200128

--- **BOOK** --

BOOK-CONS-AS CHILCOTIN WAR
  1 ea @ $9.95 /ea   9.95 G

Subtotal: 9.95
GST   0.50
Total Amount: **$10.45**

PAYMENT

Cash $20.00
Change Due $9.55

Total items: 1

a run for it or he could continue to lie in the tent hoping to avoid detection. It was unlikely the Tsilhqot'in would overlook him for long. Mosley was a hardened veteran of both the California and Cariboo gold rushes. He knew he had to make a move if he was going to live out this day.

Carefully levering himself free of the bodies of his friends, Mosley slithered out of the tent. The river was just steps away. Hauling himself to his feet, he began to run toward the water. The frantic escapee heard a shout of surprise from somewhere close behind, followed by a fusillade of gunshots. Startled by the racket, Mosley tripped on a log and tumbled over the steep bank. Sprawling over the rocks at the water's edge, oblivious to the pain, Mosley could only have marvelled that the shots—every one of them—had missed. Stumbling and gasping, he scrambled out of sight. Moments later, a Tsilhqot'in warrior approached the bank and looked up and down the river. Satisfied that one of the musket balls and the river had claimed the would-be escapee, he sauntered off.

Several hundred metres downriver, Pete Petersen had dragged himself to shore and into hiding. Not far away, Phil Buckley, bleeding heavily, reeled amongst the trees and then collapsed unconscious into the concealing underbrush.

Ed Mosley couldn't resist a glance at what was happening at the camp. Slowly peering above the riverbank, he watched women and children paw through Buttle's provision tent. Two men were dragging a body to the river. Casually, they tossed it over the bank. It hit the surface with a dull smack and disappeared beneath the swiftly moving water. Mosley slowly lowered himself down and crept away.

"Chedekki."

The packer gave a start and looked around. Klatsassin took a step toward him and then asked the unwilling warrior why he had stopped fighting.

Hadn't he done his share? After all, he had put a ball into Petersen. Unnerved, Chedekki replied, "I am standing here to stop an escape by any of the whites."

He felt his musket wrenched from his hands and turned to see Cushen holding the gun. Cushen glanced at Klatsassin. We must hurry and kill the axemen higher up the trail, he told his chief. Klatsassin nodded and the two men moved away.

"I'm no good without my gun," Chedekki called after them. "I will not go." Klatsassin and Cushen gave no indication that they even heard his words.

Chedekki stood apart from the others, watching the scene before him. Telloot, Scarface and others were busy with their knives. For a moment, it seemed that the warriors were merely ensuring every one of their enemies was dead. However, Chedekki knew the activity he was watching represented more than that. He may never have witnessed this scene before, but every Tsilhqot'in knew the ways of the tribe's warfare. These weren't the typical stabbing motions associated with inflicting mortal wounds. The Tsilhqot'in were butchering their naked victims.

9

Trail of Blood

ALFRED WADDINGTON STOOD UP AND extended his hand to Alex McDonald. Some might have been surprised that the Bute Inlet Wagon Road Company had offered a road-building contract to the backer of the Bentinck Arm route, but it was a strategic choice. Better to have McDonald work for him than against him, Waddington likely thought. Besides, McDonald knew the Chilcotin country better than anybody, except perhaps former Fort Chilcotin operator Donald McLean.

Others would not be surprised to learn that McDonald had seized the opportunity to make additional money on what would be an improvement to his pack-train route to Fort Alexandria. If "Old Waddy" wanted a road across the plateau to the Fraser, McDonald was the man to build it. The *British Columbian* could print what it wished. In these uncertain times, a wise man couldn't allow trumped-up rivalries to get in the way of a mutually beneficial business deal. And if Waddington's route failed and the Bentinck Company's succeeded, McDonald still would profit.

McDonald and his party were expected to leave Victoria for the north coast before the end of April 1864. Remembering his winter trek down the Homathko Canyon, McDonald must have smiled. Working conditions on the plateau would be a picnic compared to the hardships Brewster's poor devils were enduring in the mountains above the inlet. Waddington had called the plateau geography "more like our English parks." The old man got that right, too. For Alex McDonald, this was going to be easy money.

The Advance Party

Approximately three kilometres up the trail from the main camp, William Brewster's Homalco cook, Qwhittie, was lighting the breakfast fire for the four men who comprised the advance party of trailblazers. Accompanying Brewster was inlet settler John Clark, who had welcomed the opportunity to earn a little extra money. Brewster may have offered Clark a job as compensation for the man's troubles with the Tsilhqot'in over the winter. The other members of the group were Jim Gaudet, a mixed-blood resident of Victoria, and Baptiste Demarest, Brewster's translator.

Breakfast that day was a hurried affair. There was a lot to be accomplished. The terrain was particularly rough, and Brewster knew how critical progress was for Alfred Waddington. It's possible he also knew that they were to link up the trail as quickly as possible with McDonald's road gang, which would be working its way west toward the mountains from Puntzi Lake.

As he washed the dishes, Qwhittie could see Gaudet a short distance away, cutting away at the underbrush. Just out of sight, Clark and Demarest were busy somewhere above, doing the same. Brewster worked alone, blazing trees less than 300 metres up the trail, exposing the easily seen white wood that would indicate the proposed route.

Seconds after his axe blade had deftly peeled away the bark on a spruce tree, Brewster paused. His ears had caught a sharp, metallic click. It sounded eerily like a musket hammer falling on flint. Brewster's breath caught in his throat. A misfire? Surely not. He turned in the direction of the ominous sound.

Hidden in a concealing screen of tree limbs and leaves was an angry Tsilhqot'in. At this moment, Chessus should have been celebrating the death of another enemy. Instead, his malfunctioning weapon had betrayed him. Now the surprise was gone; the white man was on the alert. No matter. He was as good as dead anyway. Now Chessus had the pleasure of telling him so.

"We have killed the others and we are going to kill you!"

he shouted. Brewster looked frantically about him, trying to see his would-be assailant.

"Why do you want to kill me?" Brewster stammered as he backed down toward the camp. His question was answered with the crack of a musket and a white cloud of exploding powder in the brush ahead of him. Axe in hand, Brewster turned and ran down the trail as fast as he could.

Chessus followed Brewster, shoving a powder cartridge down the gun's muzzle and dropping another musket ball and wadding after it. He came to a sudden halt, seeing another target. Gaudet was so close Chessus could almost touch him. The killer crouched down and pulled at the ramrod, tamping down his weapon's charge as swiftly and silently as he could.

At the gun's blast nearby, James Gaudet had straightened up from the tangle of growth he was slashing at. Who was doing the shooting? Where had the shot come from? He had no time to formulate any answers. A second, closer shot rang out, and Gaudet's body pinwheeled with the ball's impact. Clutching his shattered shoulder, the wounded man thrashed his way down a wooded slope. Another shot boomed, and Gaudet sprawled heavily into the underbrush.

Scarface and another Tsilhqot'in were standing in the trees when John Clark burst out of the bush in front of them, running for his life. Almost simultaneously, the two warriors levelled their guns at the terrified man. The breeze whipped away the clouds of gunsmoke to reveal Clark as he crawled into the underbrush, clutching his thigh. A moment later, a hatchet caved in his skull.

Farther down the trail, a breathless Baptiste Demarest wiped the sweat from his brow and cautiously peered around the tree he was cowering behind. A hundred metres away, two Tsilhqot'in sprang into view, and Demarest didn't hesitate a second. He whirled and fled down the trail. The Tsilhqot'in stopped to take shots at him. The disbelieving warriors watched as the French-Canadian arced over the bank and into the river. They ran over and looked down into the swirling eddies below. It made no difference whether their musket balls or the river claimed him.

Qwhittie was standing near the forgotten washbasin when a Tsilhqot'in ran into the clearing, grabbed his hand and began pulling at him. Qwhittie resisted.

"You must go quickly before they kill you, too!" Qwhittie's would-be rescuer panted. "They are going to kill all the whites."

"Why do they want to kill all the whites?" Qwhittie protested.

This Tsilhqot'in had gone out of his way to try to save Qwhittie, who had befriended him some time before when he had been captured by the coastal tribe. There was no time to explain what the war chief had told them all the night before.

"I don't know," the Tsilhqot'in said, losing patience with the cook. "Go home!" Qwhittie turned and ran toward the main camp.

William Brewster crouched with his back against a large boulder and looked down at the axe still clutched in his hand. A solitary axe against so many guns! The month before as he had prepared to leave Victoria, Waddington had urged him to take more weapons. Why bother? The Indians were starving and begging for work. Who would bite the hand that fed him? Too late, Brewster now knew better.

A musket crashed and Brewster's hands clutched his chest. Half-conscious, he blinked into the looming faces of his killers, who had gathered around his slumping form. Chessus picked up Brewster's axe and raised it high over his head. He brought it down swiftly into the top of the foreman's head.

The Tsilhqot'in tore at the dead man's clothes, the axe jerking to and fro as the body was pulled about. Clutching a long, sharpened file, Chessus stuffed a severed piece of ragged flesh into Brewster's half-open mouth. Then he attacked Brewster's chest. The warriors had taken Brewster's manhood. Now they would ingest the white chief's power and that power would become theirs.

The Survivors' Stories

After he refreshed himself at a pool of rainwater, survivor Phil Buckley's first coherent thought was that he somehow had to warn Brewster. As Buckley approached the foreman's camp, he heard dogs and scurried into the underbrush. Nobody at the camp had dogs. That meant the Tsilhqot'in were still about. Soon the sounds of dancing and singing confirmed Buckley's suspicions. He carefully detoured around the ruins of the main camp and limped on down the trail.

Meanwhile, some hours after the attack, Ed Mosley and Pete Petersen had met farther down the river. In spite of Petersen's weakened condition, the two decided to head down to the ferry together. Unaware that Smith had been the first to die, the two exhausted men were confident the ferryman would assist them in getting help. Petersen collapsed before they reached the ferry and told Mosley to continue on without him. Mosley was surprised that there was no response when he shouted to Smith across the river. A few minutes later, Petersen managed to stumble down the trail to join the other survivor.

Buckley had hidden all night and caught up with Mosley and Petersen the next morning at the ferry. The former sailor used a length of hemp to hitch his way along the ferry's guy rope until he reached the other side. Fortunately, the travelling block was in working condition. Buckley sent it back to the others, and soon all three men were on the opposite side of the Homathko, where the trail continued down to the inlet. Near the ashes of Smith's fire, the survivors found a large pool of blood and a musket ball embedded in a tree that hinted at the ferryman's fate.

Over 50 kilometres of travel still lay before the three when a pair of French-Canadian packers and five Homalcos appeared in a large canoe. They had set out after

Brewster's breathless cook, Qwhittie, had stumbled into the townsite, long after Whymper and the others had left for Victoria. Qwhittie's news of the two additional attacks gave credence to Squinteye's story of Smith's killing, and a search party was organized. None of the rescuers knew it at the time, but they had already found the only survivors.

Six days after Squinteye awoke Frederick Whymper and his companions at the townsite, Victorians were reading the *Daily Chronicle* headline: RUMOURED MURDER BY AN INDIAN. Alfred Waddington undoubtedly hoped it was just a rumour. Still, it couldn't have made him very happy. Waddington didn't need any wild speculation to divert him from his travel preparations, and, more important, the Bute Inlet Wagon Road Company didn't need rumour mongers casting more aspersions on his road project.

However, the newspaper stories weren't all bad. Whymper told the *British Colonist* that the Bute trail, "pushed through fast by Mr. Brewster," was the best in the country that he had seen or travelled. The route, he reminded *Daily Chronicle* readers, was "within a 16 hours steamer-boat ride of this city, and I have no doubt that . . . this part of the country will be visited by numbers of tourists and travellers." For Waddington, these were early returns on his investment in the artist.

To Waddington's shock and horror, the rumour was finally confirmed on Wednesday morning, May 11. That morning, the steamer *Emily Harris* arrived from Nanaimo, carrying the three survivors of the Tsilhqot'in's pre-dawn attack on the Bute road party.

Waddington hurried up the steps of the Royal Hospital and was shown to the ward where the survivors lay. The men related their harrowing tales. Distraught, Waddington wanted to know why the attack had occurred. The crewmen shrugged. Who knew why Indians did what they did? Of course, no one would deny that there had been disagreements between the Tsilhqot'in and the work party, especially involving that hothead Tim Smith. But that it was petty stuff, they agreed. Ed Mosley had an idea, though.

Suppose Smith had provoked Klatsassin so much the Indian had killed him and then just gone crazy? Actually, maybe he wasn't so crazy. If he'd persuaded the others to kill everyone, Mosley went on, then who would know he had killed Smith? Nobody would be left alive to tell the tale.

The boys at the *Daily Chronicle* couldn't wait until the next scheduled edition to tell the shocking story. The newspaper published an extra edition later that day, with the headline: HORRIBLE MASSACRE!! FOURTEEN MEN MURDERED AT BUTE INLET. The newspaper had printed the rumour and was now printing the facts—facts that were more frightening than anyone could have imagined.

"There is something almost fiendish in the manner in which this treacherous massacre was perpetrated," the *British Colonist* editorialized. The Tsilhqot'in "ruthlessly shot down and savagely mutilated" crewmen who had

treated them "in the kindest manner." Despite rumours—
"but they are only rumours"—of quarrelling between Smith
and the Tsilhqot'in, the newspaper concluded that the
motive for the "treacherous atrocity of these savages" was
"entirely one of plunder."

A cynical reader would have been grimly amused at the
effusive lionization of the road builder by the usually critical *Daily Chronicle*. Alfred Waddington was now portrayed
as "an honest, patient, enterprising, self-sacrificing, noble-
hearted man" and "the good old man." But would all that
really help Waddington now?

Waddington had made his own formal deposition
before a magistrate, which was duly published in the *British
Colonist*. The actions of the Natives were a mystery, he pro-
fessed. "Telloot used to call me his best friend," he added. As
he pondered the tragedy, he took the opportunity to reflect
on another horrifying possibility. He had seen the undulat-
ing, grass-covered Chilcotin landscape with his own eyes
and could picture it again. Through the heat of the plateau
trail came the shimmering images of men approaching on
horseback. There, at the head of his road-builders' pack
train, rode Alex McDonald.

"I am very much afraid," Waddington admitted,
"the whole party will be murdered by the same Chilcotin
Indians, who appear to have gone up in their direction."

CHAPTER

10

The Bitter Truth

WHEN HE READ THE DISPATCHES from the governor of Vancouver Island at around 10 p.m. on Friday, May 13, Frederick Seymour, newly installed governor of British Columbia, likely slumped into the nearest high-backed upholstered armchair. This news of an Indian massacre in his jurisdiction was best read sitting down, preferably holding a snifter of brandy. It was the beginning of a long, exhausting night for the recent arrival from the British Honduras.

Seymour's mood quickly swung from anguish to anger. Rather than having the official dispatches delivered by a military officer, or even a government bureaucrat, for some unfathomable reason, Governor Arthur Kennedy had placed them in the hands of a civilian travelling by regular steamer. Perhaps "irregular" was a more accurate word: the *Enterprise*'s sailing had been unaccountably delayed.

Any one of the three British naval vessels idling at anchor less than 30 minutes' gallop from Kennedy's office could have sped across the strait, arriving late Wednesday, the same day the survivors arrived in Victoria. Instead, it had taken over two days for the calamitous news to reach the governor's official residence in New Westminster. Vancouver Island's delay was unconscionable.

Seymour ordered the *Enterprise* sent back to Victoria. It carried a blunt request for Kennedy to get a naval vessel over to the mainland immediately. That's all Seymour wanted from the island colony. But based on Kennedy's foot-dragging, he wondered if he could count on that much. Moreover, the killings had occurred in the mainland colony, *his* colony, and he was responsible for taking action.

The civilian who accompanied the dispatches was a certain Alfred Waddington, someone Seymour had met only briefly at his welcome dinner in Victoria. Now the Bute Inlet road builder desperately wished an audience. Seymour decided Waddington could wait on his pleasure. The governor had two other men he needed to see immediately. The first was a former governor who had years of experience with the Natives.

Recently retired James Douglas was weary and preoccupied with final preparations for a trip to England when Seymour arrived on his doorstep close to midnight.

Just three weeks on the job, BC governor Frederick Seymour faced a colonial governor's greatest nightmare: deadly attacks by the colony's Natives.

The former governor was startled to be disturbed at so late an hour and stunned at the news of the killings. What do I do now? Seymour asked.

Douglas still had a governor's decisive ways. Pick up other survivors at the inlet and investigate the site, he told Seymour. Round up a Cariboo posse—30 well-armed, mounted men should do—and travel into Chilcotin country by way of Fort Alexandria in search of the murderers. Give cash rewards for the capture of the culprits.

The second man Seymour asked to see on that long, tense night was Chartres Brew.

The Colony's Top Cop

He was called chief inspector of police, police chief or simply "judge." Frederick Seymour called him police magistrate. What Chartres Brew stood for mattered more than his title, even in the strict formality of the Victorian era. A Crimean War veteran, big, bearded Brew personified law enforcement. The English government had sent the quick-witted Irishman to the gold-rush colony in 1858. Brew estimated it would take 150 Royal Irish constables to keep the peace in the Cariboo's gold camps. The parsimonious Colonial Office in London approved a mere 15. Against all odds, Brew managed to enforce the law, while the newly installed judge, Matthew Baillie Begbie, presided over the frontier court and sentenced the lawless.

By May 1864, Brew was still keeping the peace. Desperately short of manpower, he had established the 73-man New Westminster Volunteer Rifle Corps while lobbying for arms, ammunition and, most of all, more men. The force was so short-staffed that most days there weren't enough guards to take the jail's chain gang out to repair the city's rutted streets.

When Douglas retired, Brew had decided to relinquish his onerous duties as well. However, his plans were quickly forgotten after he received Seymour's request for a meeting in the pre-dawn hours of May 14. Seymour asked Brew to lead a volunteer group to Bute Inlet, but he wanted no shooting. He would not countenance "men bent on vengeance," he later emphasized. Instead, moving up Waddington's route, Brew was instructed to "assert the supremacy of the law," and, if necessary, enter the plateau in hopes of persuading the Natives to hand over the killers. Seymour also wrote to Captain William Cox, the gold commissioner in the Cariboo town of Richfield. Cox's orders: Get a posse together and go hunt Indians.

The practical, all-purpose position of gold commissioner was one recommended by London and doubtless supported by Chartres Brew, as it relieved his small contingent of overworked police of claim registration, licensing and other gold-creek administrative duties. Nevertheless, with Brew's force spread so thinly, Cox sometimes acted as Indian agent, tax collector, justice of the peace and magistrate.

Cox's cavalier disregard for due process was well known to both Brew and Begbie. Prospectors arguing over ownership of a claim? Have them run a race and the winner takes the claim, Cox decreed. When a thief was brought before him, Cox gave the man 15 minutes to pack up, pay up and get out of town no questions asked. In another case, an angry mob rode off to Washington State to apprehend a prospector's killer and simply strung up the suspect. Outraged citizens wanted the lynch mob brought to justice, but since he didn't see the hanging, the gold commissioner said there was nothing he could do.

When informed that Cox would lead an expedition into Chilcotin country from Fort Alexandria, Brew likely put aside any worries about the gold commissioner. Hundreds of kilometres might separate Cox's expedition from his own.

Finding volunteers for the Bute Inlet force was easy. Brew had formally trained and disciplined prospects waiting for a chance to prove their worth. At least they would finally get their guns and ammunition.

Victim Becomes Villain

Standing on the deck of *Forward* as it puffed up Bute Inlet, Alfred Waddington must have agonized over the bloody demise of men in his employ and was likely weighed down with a sense of dread. What horrors awaited up the Homathko River? And what fate awaited Alex McDonald?

Waddington believed himself to be an altruistic victim, but now he felt like others held him personally responsible for the violent outbreak. In the eyes of many, Waddington feared, he was not far removed from the likes of the perpetrators themselves. In a matter of days, the unknowing victim had become the avaricious villain.

Like others, Chartres Brew probably regarded the Bute Inlet Wagon Road Company as the cause of the tragedy, rather than a victim of it. The expedition leader was cordial toward Waddington, but in a formal, even condescending way, demonstrating none of the bluff camaraderie he shared with the 28 young, excited men he had chosen from his New Westminster volunteers. The entrepreneur could not have been surprised. Brew was a by-the-book military man, not a visionary businessman. Moreover, as one of the New Westminster crowd, Brew had been as contemptuous of the Bute Inlet route as publisher John Robson.

Waddington was becoming frustrated. It had been Sunday morning before he finally met with Governor Seymour in New Westminster. His Excellency had asked Waddington for his views on capturing the murderers. Waddington offered suggestions that he later learned had already been made by James Douglas. There was one other issue, surely the greatest priority, but one nobody seemed to have considered. Waddington urged that an armed group ride up the Bentinck Trail in hopes of overtaking Alex McDonald and his men and warning them of the potential danger ahead.

Attending the meeting that Sunday morning was naval commander Lord Richard Gilford, who had only just arrived on the three-gun vessel *Forward*. Waddington turned to Gilford expectantly. Gilford's own ship was one of two 31-gun steam-powered frigates on the West Coast, big enough to transport the large force Waddington envisioned. But it was Seymour who answered for Gilford.

"Unfortunately, there is no vessel disposable," the governor said. Obviously, the two men had already conferred about naval possibilities before Waddington had arrived.

"Well, that *is* most unfortunate," Waddington shot back. He had paid the government $2,000 in various fees. That alone was enough to demand protection for his property and the men he employed.

The governor calmly assured the agitated road builder that anything more than Cox's expedition and Brew's investigation was completely unnecessary. He was confident the killings were merely an isolated incident. In his orders to Cox, he had suggested that after Brew had climbed through the mountains, "well disposed" Indians would capture and hand the murderers over to the police chief. The governor's wishful thinking must have shocked Waddington.

In the end, Seymour had asked Waddington to accompany Brew's expedition. However, just a few days later, the road builder beat a hasty retreat from Bute Inlet, leaving Brew there awaiting new orders. Waddington may later have wished he had never agreed to go in the first place. For the president of the Bute Inlet Wagon Road Company, the trip would be a nightmare, and not simply because of the gruesome discovery of what remained of foreman William Brewster and his crew.

The Grand Delusion

For veteran police chief Brew, it was not just the wrecked campsites and grisly remains of the crew that made a lasting impact. He had seen murder scenes and dead bodies before. Instead, he marvelled at the road crew's astounding naïveté, especially when "the Indians were little removed from a state of starvation." There was one exception. "The women, particularly the younger ones, were better fed than the men," he learned. This was evidence of something decidedly distasteful, as Brew knew only too well that "the price of prostitution to the hungry wretches was enough to eat."

As the employer, Waddington had been ultimately responsible for the policy of paying potential killers with guns and ammunition. "It is difficult to understand," Brew told Edward Cardwell, the secretary of state for the colonies, "how men could have such blind confidence in fickle savages as those murdered men had." Finally, about the Tsilhqot'in's murderous rampage, he concluded, "If a sound discretion had been exercised toward them, I believe this outrage would not have been perpetrated."

What Brew found most shocking was the meagre evidence of any progress on the project itself. Like most others in Victoria and New Westminster, Brew had been led to believe the road through the mountains was just a few weeks from completion. Yet, it took over seven hours for the party to make its way from the townsite to what remained of the main work camp.

"No just idea of the country of the trail can be formed from Mr. Waddington's flattering description of it," Brew wrote Seymour.

Brew had been ordered to travel through the mountains to the Chilcotin Plateau, but the woeful condition of the "trail" made the plan ludicrous. "Trails would have to be cut, bridges made, precipices scaled, and obstructions overcome," he wrote. "Within a distance of four miles, the trail crosses a mountain I consider 2,000 feet high. Mr. Waddington says 1,100. If I have to go on," he advised Seymour, "you will have to send me up horses, axes, saws and ropes."

Some of the volunteers with pack-train experience shook their heads at the notion that horses could negotiate the 140 hairpin turns in the cliff-hugging trail. As Brew and his volunteers hiked up past the main camp to the advance camp where Brewster and three others had met their violent end, they were stopped cold. Before them yawned a frightening ravine. A solitary volunteer agreed to inch his way along a 100-metre log spanning the chasm. Only then was the fate of Brewster and his party confirmed. The men were buried where they were found.

Standing on the lip of the ravine, the incredulous Brew asked Waddington how he had intended to build a road up here. "Brewster made a mistake," Waddington replied dismissively. "The trail should have been carried some other way." Brew looked about and could see no "other way" that was even remotely possible. The truth was that the road existed only in the mind of its promoter. Brew decided that Alfred Waddington was the kind of man who was "prompt to delude himself on any matter of which he makes a hobby."

11

Warpath

WILLIAM MANNING WAS SAWING LOGS when he noticed his Tsilhqot'in klootchman, Nancy, whispering with a couple of other Native women near the house. He put down the heavy crosscut saw and took a drink of cool water, watching the other two women scurry away into the aspen trees. When Nancy approached, Manning could see the concern etched in her face. He asked her what the two women had told her.

"The Tsilhqot'in have killed all the whites at Homathko and will come and kill you," Nancy replied.

Was it true? Manning hadn't forgotten the confrontation at the spring. Yet, he had shared his crops with these people.

"I don't believe the Tsilhqot'in will hurt me," he told Nancy. "I've known them for a long time now. They like me." Then, perhaps in an effort to convince himself, he added, "They have given me the land."

Nancy realized then that Manning had misunderstood. It wasn't Tahpit's Puntzi Lake Tsilhqot'in she was talking about. They hadn't killed the whites. "These Tsilhqot'in come from a distance. I don't know them." Nancy began to back away from Manning. "I'm afraid. I want to go."

Manning told her to get back inside and finish cooking. When he was finished eating, he walked outside to begin work again. He did not notice the old Tsilhqot'in woman walk swiftly through the clearing and slip through the open doorway behind him. Inside the cool, dim interior of the house, the visitor spoke quietly to Nancy. Trouble was coming, she insisted. "Maybe they'll kill you, too. You better go away."

Taking Revenge

Not far away, Tahpit snatched up his musket and strode out of his Puntzi Lake village. He had taken enough. For two days, visiting chief Anahim had been nagging at him constantly to kill Manning. Soon, others were taunting him, too.

Things had been peaceful enough until Klatsassin had visited and fired them all up with his tales of wiping out the whites at Bute Inlet. If they wanted Tahpit to show them what a Tsilhqot'in could do, he would show them.

Tahpit's hope that Anahim would leave him in peace once he left his village was immediately dashed. Anahim and a gaggle of others followed along close behind, eager to see if the frustrated man had what it took to kill the enemy. It probably never occurred to Tahpit to ask Anahim why *he* didn't kill Manning, if he felt so strongly about it. One did not challenge a greater chief.

Up ahead, three women were gathering firewood as Tahpit strode past. One looked up in curiosity. "Where are you going?" she asked.

"They urge me to kill Manning," Tahpit grunted, without slacking his pace. The women dropped their bundles of wood and joined the others traipsing behind him.

Another Tsilhqot'in woman from the village hurried ahead, unseen. A few minutes later, she stumbled breathlessly into the ranch house, startling Nancy. "Come with me," the rescuer gasped. "And don't stop!" Nancy followed the woman out the door and ran into the tall grass.

"Mr. Manning."

At the sound of the voice behind him, the rancher straightened up, turned and saw Tahpit level his gun at him. The force of the musket ball entering his chest threw Manning back a step, and he landed heavily on his back. Before Manning had stopped moving, Tahpit had dropped his gun, fumbled under his blanket for his hatchet and approached the helpless man. Straddling Manning's torso, Tahpit brought the hatchet down twice into his face.

At the sound of the gunshot, Nancy stopped and dashed back in the direction of the house. There, in the trees, she watched the men kick Manning's limp form, and the women squabble over items from inside the house. Others were breaking up the plow. Quietly, Nancy stepped across a yard strewn with boxes and cooking utensils and went inside the house to retrieve her belongings. There was nothing left to take.

As Nancy emerged from the house, her brother came forward. Together, they dragged Manning's body to the shallows of the stream and covered it with branches. As she walked away, Nancy noticed Tahpit slumped nearby. His face was buried in a corner of his blanket, and he was sobbing uncontrollably.

A Frightening Story

The singing and dancing that began in front of Manning's blazing house continued days later at Nancootlem. It was a time of stories, celebration and preparation for brave deeds to come. Old Anahim sat quietly observing the young war chief who had so galvanized his followers. Because this was a time of war, Klatsassin—not Chief Anahim—was the focus of attention. Anahim accepted this and bore Klatsassin no ill will. Besides, the war chief had proven to be useful.

Through Klatsassin's influence, Anahim had been able to persuade Tahpit to get rid of that pest Manning. Now, Klatsassin was making exciting plans. On the other side of the lake, men leading a loaded pack train had pulled up to rest. Anahim realized what a wonderful opportunity the pack train's arrival represented. The war chief could lead the Tsilhqot'in people into battle on *this* side of the mountains.

Rank and privilege assured Anahim a share of the spoils.

At Nancootlem, packer Peter "Mac" McDougall's young klootchman, Klymtedza, had come to visit. Often on the trail or in Bella Coola, Klymtedza was seldom seen in Nancootlem any more, but she saw her family whenever she could. She was there because she was travelling with McDougall in the pack train now resting across the lake. Mesmerized by Klatsassin, the excited warriors paid her no heed.

Klymtedza was shocked by Klatsassin's stories of death and destruction. When she heard his plans to attack her own white man and the others, she dashed back to the pack train. The panicked woman's story came out in a confusion of broken English, Chinook and Tsilhqot'in. McDougall thought the story was an exaggeration; nevertheless, he called the pack train's leader over to listen to the tale.

Alex McDonald was sobered by the story of murder and mayhem in the Homathko Canyon. There were too many telling details for it to be a total fabrication. The crew—including Malcolm McLeod—were chilled by the prospect that William Manning might have been killed up the trail at the Puntzi Lake ranch. That story also had the ring of truth. Two years before, McLeod's brother and McDonald's cousin, Robert, had been killed near the lake leading a pack train just like theirs.

McDonald made a swift decision. The men moved up to a nearby knoll, hobbled the horses in protective trees and began to dig out a rifle pit. After a period of frenzied work, McDonald, his young Tsilhqot'in servant, Tom, and his seven pack-train companions, including two would-be Cariboo prospectors, John Grant and Clifford Higgins, settled into their chest-high earthworks, guns at the ready.

The End of the Trail

Two long and uneventful days later, the impatient men huddled together to decide what to do next. Some wanted to go on to Puntzi Lake. Mac conferred quickly with Klymtedza. She was sure they would be cut to ribbons trying to ride past the lake to distant Fort Alexandria. Her advice was to ride back to Bella Coola as fast as they could. Leave the pack animals and their loads, she told him. Speed was everything.

McDonald agreed to return north and down to the coast. But leave the horses and supplies for the Tsilhqot'in? Not a chance. Moving quickly, the men repacked the animals. Within a few minutes, with Higgins, McDougall and Klymtedza in the lead, the heavily loaded pack train trotted noisily down the trail.

Later that day, Klymtedza grew frightened. Tsilhqot'in were running through the stunted spruce on the side of the trail, she told McDougall. They had no trouble keeping pace with the slow-moving group. Nobody else could see anything. Leave the horses, the frantic woman urged. Get into the woods!

McDonald ignored her, moving the group on down the trail. The tension mounted as fearful eyes darted into the trees on either side of the trail. An interminable hour crawled by. Then, a volley of gunshots shattered the silence.

McDougall's hands flew to his chest. "My God, I'm shot!" he grunted, and toppled from his saddle. Another bullet found Clifford Higgins, and he fell to the ground. With a scream, Klymtedza jumped from her mount and raced over to her fallen Mac. There were more shots, and she staggered and collapsed into the grass.

When his horse whinnied in sudden pain, McDonald threw himself clear as the beast thrashed about at the side of the trail. With one hand, he slid his shotgun from its scabbard. Turning from his stricken horse, he reached out for the flying reins of McDougall's whirling mount and vaulted into the empty saddle.

Extricating himself from under his fallen horse, John Grant looked up at McDonald. Lucky man, a good horse under him; he could still escape. The rest of them were doomed. "Go! Go!" Grant shouted.

McDonald fought to control the terrified horse, and cocked the hammers on his shotgun. "I'll give them all I have first!" he shouted and levelled the barrels in the direction of the gunsmoke drifting between the trees. The gun boomed.

Malcolm McLeod aimed his rifle at his assailants. Before he could pull the trigger, a ball gouged his hand to the bone. His rifle tumbled to the ground. A moment later, his horse shuddered, and McLeod rolled free of the collapsing animal.

Loaded horses plunged and reared. Taking advantage

of the panicking animals, Grant and others, including McLeod, dashed for the trees. Grant felt a musket ball rip into his arm, but barely slowed his pace. Another man made for a small pond. In the precious moments it took for his pursuers to reload their muskets, he tossed his hat into the water and dove into nearby bushes. The ruse saved his life.

In the trees, safe from the shotgun's blast, Klatsassin's son, Piell, took aim at Alex McDonald's horse. A moment later, his second mount shot out from under him, the pack-train leader was running for cover. More shots crashed out, and he skidded along the ground, hit in both legs.

Wounded in three places, a breathless John Grant peered out between the bushes at McDonald, who was using his elbows to drag himself along on his back toward a big tree. Grant watched in horror as a Tsilhqot'in warrior raced toward the stricken man. McDonald paused and calmly fired his six-gun, sending the warrior flying backwards into the bush. Grant had seen enough and stumbled away.

Sitting behind the tree, his legs bleeding profusely, McDonald coolly held off his attackers, taking slow, deliberate aim with his revolver at any movement. Finally, his handgun empty, McDonald reached for his shotgun. If he could just jam the shells into the open barrels . . . Another shot pierced both his arms. When McDonald looked up, a pair of cold blue eyes in a clean-shaven face stared back at him. Who are *you*? the dying man might have wondered. Klatsassin raised his rifle and shot the pack-train leader through the head.

112

12

Manhunt

ALFRED WADDINGTON, AMOR DE COSMOS and the dozen others on the stage could not have hoped for a better turnout. The Victoria Theatre was packed. Mayor Tom Harris introduced De Cosmos, who walked to the rostrum and looked out over an audience hushed in anticipation.

"I regard the occasion which called this meeting together as one from which none should flinch," De Cosmos began gravely. Eager to reinforce his reputation as a far-sighted man of vision, he said "I believe I was one of the first to have mooted the subject of the Bute Inlet Route," but "I did not then think that I should be compelled to express the feelings of the community at such outrages." Then, in recognition of the true visionary in their midst, he continued, "This meeting should express its sympathy to Mr. Waddington, for I believe that worthy gentleman is not only entitled to sympathy but also to compensation for the losses which have overtaken him through the acts of these savages."

Just the afternoon before, "the feelings of the community" were decidedly more ambivalent. Inside the Victoria Rifle Corps drill hall, an emotional civilian attending a meeting was greeted with roars of laughter when he announced he was ready to "murder every Indian he could lay his hands on!" However, that was before other citizens took the threat of Native violence seriously enough to petition Mayor Harris to convene a more formal meeting on June 2. With the city's mayor and Member of the Assembly lending it the stamp of officialdom, and aided by the newspapers' accounts of the McDonald pack-train attack, anxious citizens filled the theatre.

Thanks to "the murder of a number of our fellow countrymen," as he put it to the riveted crowd, De Cosmos' political destiny was unfolding as he undoubtedly felt it should. Now an elected member of the House and former newspaper editor (he had finally won a seat and sold the *British Colonist* the year before), De Cosmos likely welcomed this opportunity to redeem himself with his constituents.

In what appeared a fiscally prudent decision, De Cosmos had helped defeat a motion to finance the construction of a home for the island colony's new governor, Arthur Kennedy, and to pay the salary of his private secretary. Let London foot those bills, the House decided. However, Victorians, eager to demonstrate their loyalty to the new governor, were outraged over what many considered unforgivable slights. "The most wanton piece of discourtesy," the *British Colonist* huffed. Both De Cosmos and the Speaker were shouted down when they attempted to explain their actions in a special meeting. Now, in the very same theatre, De Cosmos had taken the stage again, anxious to win the public's favour.

"Our treatment of the Indians should be this," De Cosmos instructed the audience, "whenever life is taken, blood should be taken in return. The Indian knows no law but blood for blood!" The crowd erupted in cheers.

When pressed, De Cosmos likely would have clarified that by "the Indians" he meant only those actually guilty of perpetrating the attack. At this point, it seemed most people in Victoria and New Westminster were willing to consider a more judicial approach. The *Daily Chronicle* stated, "With returning reason, however, the public are willing to discriminate between the innocent and guilty." The pragmatic *British Columbian* suggested, "Indiscriminate slaughter would not mend, but aggravate the matter."

The day after the public meeting, De Cosmos headed a special citizens' committee that met with the new governor to ask him to sanction a volunteer expedition. Sorry, Kennedy told them, the killings occurred on the mainland. He had to wait for an invitation from Governor Frederick Seymour in New Westminster, but would write to him to offer assistance. In the meantime, he advised, "Every man in the colony should know how to handle a rifle."

Seymour sent back a curt reply: "The time may perhaps come when I may have to call for their services, but it has not yet arrived." British Columbia was *his* colony, and he alone would protect its citizens.

The bureaucratic sidestepping exasperated Victoria citizens. Over the next few weeks, city newspapers advocated a forthright kill-them-all approach. "Had the people of Victoria had the power," the *Daily Chronicle* fumed, "they would gladly have exterminated the whole tribe to which the murderers belong." Counselled the *British Colonist*: "An armed hunting party should be formed to mete out that justice-by-rope . . . Let them not stay their hands until every member of the rascally murderers' tribe is suspended from the trees of their own forests."

Indian-Hunter

About the time Seymour was declining Victoria's offer of volunteers, Donald McLean and his son Duncan were waiting at the end of the Cariboo wagon road at Soda Creek for Gold Commissioner Cox's volunteers from Williams, Lightning and Antler creeks. They had expected Cox to step off the river steamer from Quesnellemouth for days now. McLean—second in command—had acted quickly when he got the word and had rounded up 23 men and 100 guns.

Eight years before, the gold nugget McLean saw on his

Fort Kamloops counter had told him that the company was living on borrowed time. Managing horses and cattle for HBC forts gave McLean the background he needed to strike out on his own. In 1860, with his third wife—a Tsilhqot'in he called Sophia—and his many children, McLean established a ranch at Hat Creek. McLean's roadhouse and restaurant, located at the end of the new stage line, now fed and housed prospectors anxious to reach Cariboo gold creeks to the north.

Impatient with Cox's delay, McLean was ready to pack up when he got word that William Manning had been cut down at Puntzi. That was enough to move him to write to the governor, assuring him that he would expend "utmost efforts to secure the object of the expedition."

That object was to bring the "rascally murderers" to justice. It was nothing new for McLean. Fifteen years before, he had led a posse after a member of the Quesnel band called Tlhelh, who had shot and killed a company translator. McLean tracked the killer down in his village at the site of Quesnellemouth. Angered by the chief, whom he believed was harbouring the fugitive, McLean yelled, "Then for today, you'll be Tlhelh," pulled two pistols and began blasting away. His guns empty, he grabbed his musket. When it was over, McLean had killed the chief, his son-in-law and infant grandchild and wounded his daughter-in-law.

Respected by white settlers, traders and prospectors, to whom he represented law and order, the chief trader was reviled by the Natives. He began wearing a chain-mail vest, and over the years the myth grew that no bullet could stop Donald McLean.

Finally, Cox's force arrived by raft. The steamer had been knocked out of commission, so Cox had improvised. His ragtag mob of adventure-seeking traders and prospectors sported names like "Six-Toed Pete" and "Wild Yankee." Recruiting had been easy. Most of the threadbare volunteers would earn more on the trail than on the creeks.

Together with McLean's men, Cox's group crossed the Fraser at Fort Alexandria, and the combined forces rode out into Chilcotin country. Two days later, Cox demonstrated his unorthodox leadership when one miner pulled a knife on another. Cox intervened and gave the guilty party 10 minutes to get his gear and make it back to Alexandria—if he could. No, he could *not* take a horse, Cox told him. He would have to take his chances on foot. It was a sobering lesson for the rough-and-tumble volunteers.

Cox respected McLean's legendary savvy, and told him that he would follow his suggestions. However, it wasn't long before Cox was exercising full control.

On Sunday, June 12, four days after leaving Fort Alexandria, Cox and McLean reached Manning's gutted ranch house and uncovered his body. McLean read the burial service. Later, acting as scouts, McLean and his son observed a large Tsilhqot'in village (probably Tahpit's) and rode back to tell Cox. McLean suggested they surround the village, which would make it easy to round up the suspected murderers. Cox had another plan: a theatrical show of force on the hill overlooking the village, designed to frighten the Tsilhqot'in into submission. McLean knew better but had little choice other than to go along with the plan. As soon as the Tsilhqot'in saw the armed group on the hill, they fled in panic. Mindful of Seymour's admonition to avoid a "collision" with the Natives, Cox allowed them to escape, much to McLean's annoyance. They would question no suspects that day and pondered what to do next.

Cox had no passion for riding around in the bush. McLean suggested that he, his son Duncan and others would do the riding, find the Tsilhqot'in chief Alexis, and ask him where the murderers were hiding. McLean felt he could move faster and more efficiently without Cox's ignorant rabble, so off they went. That night, some distance away, Klatsassin himself was watching the whites at their campfires.

The force's Native trackers told Cox's party that Tsilhqot'in were close by. Soon, their suspicions were confirmed. Eager for action, Cox's men dashed off in pursuit. Hiding in a wooded area, Tsilhqot'in warriors opened fire on the confused, frightened men, wounding one before melting away into the trees. Cox wasn't about to put any more men at risk, so his Indian-hunters were ordered to build a crude fort to protect themselves from attack. For good measure, he ordered the Puntzi Lake village burned to the ground.

Three days later, McLean rejoined Cox. He had met

with Alexis' band and had good news. The murderers were somewhere to the west, between Puntzi Lake and Bute Inlet. Better still, Alexis would come to Cox. After hanging a flag of truce, Cox decided to sit and wait for the chief's arrival. Weeks later, he was still waiting.

The Governor Marches In

While Cox relaxed and McLean fretted, down in Burke Channel the smoke and thunder from the screw frigate *Sutlej*'s 35 guns sent the Nuxalk fleeing into the forest. Their culture already shattered by smallpox, the cacophony from the ships appeared to signal the end of the world. In fact, it merely heralded His Excellency, Governor Seymour, who had journeyed up the coast with Chartres Brew.

After conferring with three of the five survivors of McDonald's pack train, Seymour realized that he might have been able to prevent the attack had Kennedy given him the naval support he had originally requested. Now all they could do was bury the dead and track down the killers.

Up the trail they marched, over 75 strong, leading 19 horses. Days later, as they approached deserted Nancootlem, they were met by a welcoming committee sent by Cox. Operators of a supply train from Fort Alexandria had told Cox that Seymour and Brew were making for Bella Coola and would ride south down the plateau. The governor was given a note from Cox politely suggesting that he didn't need Brew and advising them to

Chartres Brew's "stiff upper lip" composure was sorely tested as he and his exhausted men faced starvation.

turn back. The Fort Alexandria volunteers could bring in the Tsilhqot'in. Seymour thought otherwise.

For the governor, the Native uprising was a wonderful opportunity to inspire fear—or at least respect—in the Natives. Besides, he had never seen the Cariboo. Once there, he could impress everyone on the Fraser and the prospectors on the creeks, too. He would march on.

A few days later, Seymour and Brew found the site of the McDonald ambush. For Brew, it was the Bute Inlet horror all over again: mangled human remains riddled with bullet holes and half-eaten by wolves. Added to the evil-smelling carnage were the fly-infested, bloated bodies of horses. A volunteer burial party set to work.

On Wednesday, July 6, the two expeditionary forces met at Puntzi Lake. The volunteers mingled, comparing stories and discussing the idiocy of their leaders. The meeting between the leaders themselves was something quite different.

The Death of a Legend

Frederick Seymour was disgusted. For three weeks, William Cox and his men had sat around Puntzi Lake accomplishing virtually nothing. The next day, he sent them south to the mountains to track the renegades. Chartres Brew shared the governor's disgust. But Brew likely was not surprised. The difference in the two groups had become apparent their first night together. Long after Brew's disciplined former Royal Engineers were already in their tents, Cox's rabble contin-ued to laugh, drink, play cards and dance about.

Meanwhile, Donald McLean was exasperated almost beyond reason. Days after he had left the lake, he had come close to engaging the Tsilhqot'in several times. Shots had been exchanged, and Klatsassin had been spotted on one occasion, but the chief and his war party had eluded them every time. With his miner–Indian hunters impatient for action, Cox decided to return to Puntzi Lake. McLean, however, decided to give it one more try. On the morning of July 17, he prodded a Native guide, Jack, awake. Together the two walked quickly and quietly out of the sleeping camp.

Klatsassin's scouts were out early that morning, too. One watched from a hiding place, his rifle levelled at the two men moving slowly up a small ravine. He saw the guide tug on the white man's sleeve.

"Indians near," Jack whispered. McLean leaned his gun up against a rock and mopped his brow. The day was going to be a scorcher. Jack wanted to turn back. That was typical, McLean must have thought, just when they were close to what they'd been looking for.

"Don't be foolish, Jack. We'll be alright," he admonished. The two men moved on.

As he passed a clump of screening trees, McLean stopped short, raised his gun and cocked the hammer. He whirled around, expecting to see a gun barrel protruding from the branches. Instead, there was nothing. Instinctively, Jack could feel someone in the brush behind McLean's back and threw himself to the ground. An instant later, there was a deafening roar and Donald McLean went down. A second shot quickly followed, the ball whistling over Jack's head. The guide jumped to his feet and raced down the trail.

A few seconds later, Jack almost collided with the camp lookout, who had heard the shots and come galloping up. The two men returned to McLean. There was nothing they could do; the chain mail hadn't protected McLean's back. The legendary trader, vigilante and pioneer rancher was dead. McLean's son, Duncan, ran up from camp. Distraught at the sight of his dead father, Duncan cocked his revolver and raised it to his head. Quick hands grappled for the weapon, and Duncan fainted.

Within minutes, Cox and his volunteers filed up the trail. Cox ordered a detachment to carry McLean's body back to camp, then led the others up to the crown of a nearby hill. From there, Klatsassin and six followers were spotted through a telescope. Muskets barked and Klatsassin and his men bolted. Cox had ordered the hill surrounded, but the desperate Tsilhqot'in chose a risky jump from a perpendicular bluff into a lagoon below and swam through the encircling volunteers. They had escaped once again.

Surrender

At last, there was something both Chartres Brew and William Cox agreed on. On July 20, short of food and exhausted from weeks of fruitless searching, both leaders approached Governor Seymour and suggested they give up. Seymour would have none of it. With McLean dead and another wounded, the situation had deteriorated since his arrival. The governor decreed that he would leave for Fort Alexandria, as planned, but he ordered Brew to find the killers and Cox and his men to stay at Puntzi Lake.

Brew was disappointed; he felt any hunt was doomed to

failure. Cox was humiliated and now wanted to continue the hunt. Angry miners demanded that they be allowed to hunt Indians or they would go back to the Cariboo. In later correspondence with Cardwell, the usually diplomatic Seymour recalled his mood during those frustrating days at Puntzi Lake: "There was no use shutting my eyes to the fact that this was war . . . Happily for the occasion, our Constables knew the use of rifle and revolver at least as well [as the Tsilhqot'in]." Later, he bluntly stated, "I may find myself compelled to follow in the footsteps of the Governor of Colorado . . . and invite every white man to shoot each Indian he may meet. Such a proclamation would not be badly received here."

Quite unexpectedly, the camp had a visitor. Chief Alexis had decided to come calling. Seymour had not yet departed, so when armed Tsilhqot'in galloped up and Alexis loudly demanded to see the Great Chief, the governor himself stepped forward. The parlay that followed did not go well. Alexis disavowed Klatsassin's actions, calling the killers "some bad savages," and said his people had nothing to do with any of the murders. He also heaped scorn on the whites.

Long after Alexis announced he'd talked enough and abruptly stalked off to sleep, Seymour agonized over a way to win the chief's confidence. He was shaving the next morning when others ran up and gave him the word that the contemptuous Tsilhqot'in were leaving. Wiping lather from his face, Seymour strode out to the chief. Explaining he was moving out to Fort Alexandria, Seymour had an uncharacteristic moment of inspiration. Would Alexis accompany him to offer his group safety on the trail? Flattered at the Great Chief's respect and trust, Alexis quickly agreed.

Relieved that a crisis had been averted and that provisions had arrived from Bella Coola, Seymour decided to allow Cox to continue the search. Alexis' group would accompany Cox, who was sure to feed them. The chief assured Seymour he would send word to guarantee his safety on the trail to Fort Alexandria. Brew and his volunteers were ordered north to Anahim's territory. A few days later, Puntzi Lake was deserted.

As Cox's group approached the ruins of Fort Chilcotin, Tahpit's son arrived with a message from Klatsassin. Stop where you are, he warned, or we'll wipe you out. Cox's return message was unequivocal. The Tsilhqot'in were welcome to come to him. If not, the gold commissioner warned, "I will follow them up and kill every man, woman and child." Then, Cox returned to his favourite strategy: sitting and waiting.

After two weeks of fruitless searching, Chartres Brew and his exhausted, hungry men—at times reduced to eating roots and berries—were back at Puntzi Lake enjoying long-awaited provisions. With the food came news that the police chief must have found hard to take: Klatsassin had surrendered to William Cox. Brew had no time to waste on bitter thoughts of that disrespectful dilettante basking in glory. There were other fugitives to bring to justice.

CHAPTER

13

Aftermath

ANAHIM WAS VISITING THE Bella Coola Valley when he heard about the relentless search for Klatsassin's warriors. The whites were looking for him, too, so he decided it would be prudent to offer them some help and hand over eight horses given to him by Klatsassin from the McDonald pack train. Early in September, half a dozen of Brew's men met Anahim's group on the trail above the Bella Coola River. They exchanged gifts and all returned to Nancootlem.

When the chief arrived at the village, Brew was waiting. He hadn't found anything that directly linked Anahim to the ambush of McDonald's party. Brew questioned the cagey chief, but he insisted he didn't know much. He offered to look for the remaining fugitives, and Brew agreed. A few days later, the chief was back with even more of McDonald's livestock but no prisoners. Anahim promised to keep looking.

Close to starvation, Anahim's people began to eat their horses. Brew gave them food and a note entitling them to more from the store at Bella Coola. When the men awoke one morning, there was snow on their blankets. It was time, the police chief thought, to end his expedition. On September 29, his gaunt and haggard force reached Bella Coola. They had been gone from New Westminster 107 days. At least Brew could console himself that the governor would be happy.

"That Europeans should thus run down wild Indians," Seymour later wrote, "and drive them to suicide or surrender in their own hunting grounds in the fruit and fish season, appears to me, I confess, a little short of marvellous."

Anger and Outrage

Klatsassin would never forget Cox's reply, brought back by the slave he had captured from McDonald's pack train. Cox would not harm them if they came in, the slave told him. Cox would simply "hand them over to the Big Chief." Klatsassin took that to mean Governor Seymour—and with good reason. At Cox's camp, someone had shown the slave Seymour's picture.

The war chief weighed his options. There were too many white men and too many guns. Worse, Anahim had not joined him as Klatsassin had hoped. Scouts told him that Alexis had been talking with the whites. There was no help there. When the whites had marched onto the plateau from the coast, the Tsilhqot'in were stunned to see Nuxalk warriors in their ranks, looking like fools in their blue uniforms. Klatsassin and his followers were now alone. And they were tired. Their women and children were frightened, and everyone was hungry. The marauding white men would soon control the fishing grounds. What would they eat when winter came? Klatsassin's wife had just given birth to a daughter. What future did their children have? Telloot and Tahpit argued that surrender would not mean death but simply that the war would end. So, on the morning of August 15, Klatsassin and seven others had walked into Cox's camp, unarmed, wives and children in tow.

Leaving the women and children some distance away, the Tsilhqot'in men sat on the ground and Klatsassin began to speak. Cox's translator cocked an ear.

"I have brought seven murderers," the translator relayed to Cox, "and I am one myself. We wish to give ourselves to you to save our wives and our children."

The Tsilhqot'in realized that some of the armed white men had circled behind them, but they were not concerned. Cox was talking again, very slowly and sombrely. The translator began to speak.

"I wish to inform you that in the name of the Queen, I am placing you under arrest," he said. "You are my prisoners."

Klatsassin was stunned. "Where is Great Chief English?" he demanded, meaning the governor. His question went unanswered.

"King George's men are great liars!" Telloot shouted.

The eight men were bound at gunpoint and sur-rounded by guards while others hastily erected a stout wooden stockade to serve as a wilderness prison. Alexis, who had expected they would have their own camp and enjoy relaxed meals with their families, was outraged. The promise of a meeting with Seymour had meant nothing. "Many white men claim to be chiefs," Alexis had sneered to Seymour when he had first met him weeks before. "We do not know who to trust any longer." Now he, too, had allowed himself to be fooled.

Once led into the stockade, Klatsassin went wild with grief and humiliation. He had betrayed his people. He hammered his head against the posts and clawed at his face. Volunteers placed him in manacles. Some wondered what could have set him off so violently. Others who had heard the parlay guessed the answer lay in the difference between "Great Chief" (Seymour) and "Big Chief" (Judge Begbie). Had Cox tricked the war chief into surrendering? And perhaps some who witnessed the surrender might have wondered: what man calls himself a "murderer"?

* * *

Upon reading of Chartres Brew's meeting with Anahim, Alfred Waddington was incensed. Brew had the culprit in the palm of his hand and then let him go free! Many suspected Anahim had been directly involved in the

McDonald attack. "And he was still more strongly suspected of having taken an indirect part," Waddington complained. The ambush had taken place in Anahim's territory, he noted, and the chief had taken a great portion of the spoils.

"I cannot say that such was not the case," Brew conceded. However, he was certain Anahim did not learn of the attack until some days afterward, and, according to the Tsilhqot'in he talked with, "If Anahim had been at home Aleck [sic] McDonald would not have been attacked."

Another issue had Waddington seething. He had decided to sell his rights to the road to the government. He calculated his losses and projected earnings and suggested $100,000 would be a fair asking price. The Attorney General politely informed Waddington that a charter had yet to be granted. Waddington was incredulous. "Charter" was often synonymous with "agreement for charter," the Attorney General explained, but a charter could not be granted until the road had been made. Alas, there was no road; therefore, Waddington had nothing to sell.

Trial and Prosecution
When six Tsilhqot'in appeared before Matthew Baillie Begbie in Quesnellemouth, the judge was well aware of the circumstances that had brought them there. He had been at Richfield when Cox mustered his men for the manhunt.

Begbie, who wore the formal robes of court even in the humblest of settings, was no stranger to the difficult task of applying formal English law to people who had no under-standing of civilization's legal concepts.

Yes, Cox maintained in his hearing testimony, the Tsilhqot'in knew very well that surrender meant their arrest, and that they would be tried for their crimes. Given the "understanding" of the Native peoples, Begbie doubted Cox's assertion. However, the validity of the charges rested on the concept of inducement. Were the Tsilhqot'in offered an inducement to surrender? If so, the judge would have to throw out the suspects' confessions, and they would be set free.

"There was no inducement whatsoever held out to the Indians to come in," Cox argued. Knowing Cox's laissez-faire attitude and the circumstances of the manhunt, the troubled judge decided to interview Klatsassin himself.

Begbie ducked through the doorway of the makeshift log jail where the prisoners had been shackled to the wall for a month. Inside the dim, foul-smelling room, Begbie, who spoke the Tsilhqot'in's northern Athapaskan tongue, asked the war chief, "Would you have come in if you had known that you would be in confinement up to your trial before me, and to be dealt with then for the murder of these men?"

"No," Klatsassin replied.

"You had no flour," Begbie continued. "You could not hunt. You had no fish. You could not light a fire. Must you not have come in soon on any terms?"

"Yes," Klatsassin admitted.

Judge Matthew Baillie Begbie worried that the Tsilhqot'in might escape the hangman through a technicality and decided to interview them in their log prison.

Good enough, the judge decided.

In just two days, six men were tried in four separate trials. Telloot, Klatsassin and three others, including Chessus and Piell, were charged with the attempted murder of Phil Buckley. Chessus, Piell and Chedekki were charged with aiding and abetting. Actual evidence against Klatsassin was weak, Begbie admitted, but the jury had to be satisfied that "all accused were acting in concert." Buckley's own testimony made a strong impact, and Klatsassin and Telloot were convicted. The other three were acquitted but would appear in later trials in New Westminster, where it was expected that the testimony of Pete Petersen would send Chedekki to the gallows.

Tahpit was tried for the murder of William Manning, and it was Nancy's testimony that doomed him.

"These are lies!" Tahpit shouted. "I did not wish to kill, but Anahim forced me by threats." However, when another Tsilhqot'in woman testified against him, Tahpit admitted, "The words of this woman are right."

Jury members had no way of knowing what Tahpit was saying about Anahim. The judge understood, but withheld the translation of Tahpit's incriminating remarks from the jury. It didn't matter. The jury, composed of white men, convicted Tahpit of murder without even leaving the jury box.

Klatsassin and his son, Piell, stood trial for McDonald's murder. The verdict was guilty. Chessus was later found guilty of the murder of Waddington settler John Clark.

Begbie always remembered Klatsassin, whom he described at the time as "the finest savage I have met with yet." Nevertheless, he added, "I believe he has fired more shots than any of them."

The judge asked the five who were found guilty what Tsilhqot'in law was against murderers.

"Death," the men replied.

"Our law, just the same," Begbie answered.

"It seems horrible to hang five men at once—especially under the circumstances of the capitulation," Begbie admitted to the Attorney General. "Yet the blood of twenty-one whites calls out for retribution."

As he left for New Westminster, Begbie asked Anglican priest Reverend R.C. Lundin Brown to "instruct them" and even offered to use his influence to ensure he had sufficient time to do so before their execution.

"Five criminals to be prepared for eternity! Here was a definite piece of work cut out for one," Brown confessed, but it was work "more practicable, seemingly, than promiscuous preaching to gold diggers." For days, Brown, who had previously met Klatsassin (who had shown him the wooden cross he wore—a gift from a Roman Catholic priest), worked hard to persuade the five to see the error of their ways and to beg Christ for forgiveness. Thou shalt not kill, he reminded them.

"We meant war, not murder," they replied.

"Was it war," Brown asked, "to fall upon a man who was at peace with you, to massacre him in his house, in the night, to cut down his tent pole, and break his head? That was murder, surely, not war," he concluded, perhaps unaware that these strategies had typified war between BC's Native peoples for generations.

The execution at Quesnellemouth attracted miners from miles around, and a newlywed couple from near Williams Lake made the trip to witness the hangings. On the cold morning of October 26, a crowd of 250 watched as nooses were tightened around the necks of all five prisoners. All but Chessus, who was defiant to the end, prayed quickly and quietly, using words Brown had taught them.

"Have courage!" Tahpit shouted to his companions. Then he yelled, "Tell the Tsilhqot'in to cease their anger against the whites. We are going to see the Great Father!"

The men were blindfolded. With a clatter, five traps in the wooden platform simultaneously sprang open.

Ten months later, two other Klatsassin followers were tried in New Westminster for the murder of Peter McDougall. Governor Seymour pardoned one, deciding that there had been "enough life sacrificed already." Not quite enough, however, to keep the second Tsilhqot'in prisoner, Ahan, from meeting the hangman at the rear of the jail.

Somewhere between Quesnellemouth and New Westminster, Chedekki escaped and was never recaptured. Several others, including Cushen and the warrior who shot the legendary Donald McLean, were never apprehended.

The Dreamer Dreams On

The choice of superintendent of education was a good one. Alfred Waddington was an educated man and an experienced, gifted administrator. Waddington swallowed his pride and took the job in 1865. The government position kept him in the public eye, and the paycheque bought him time, and time, it appeared, was on the dreamer's side.

Amor De Cosmos, now premier of the newly created province of British Columbia, began to campaign hard for union with Canada. The confederation bargaining chip was a national railroad. Thus, both political intrigue and the railroad made the two old men brothers-in-arms once again.

Tireless Waddington spread the word that Bute Inlet was the preferred western railroad terminus. He told Americans. He told the British. In February 1872, he was in Ottawa telling the government's railway builders the same thing. One afternoon, while meeting with railway officials, Waddington was introduced to a late-arriving physician who, shaking his hand warmly, excused his tardiness by saying, "I have just left the worst case of confluent smallpox I have ever seen!"

Shocked at the doctor's foolhardiness, Waddington immediately extracted his hand. A few days later, the railroad promoter was vomiting and shaking with fever. On February 26, Alfred Waddington died, a victim of the disease that had killed so many others caught up in what history would finally call the Chilcotin War.

The 21st Century

ON OCTOBER 26, 1999, THE 135TH anniversary of the Quesnellemouth hangings, over 200 spectators gathered near where the graves of Klatsassin and his followers were thought to be for a formal government apology and the instalment of a plaque commemorating the five men who were hanged. It took a government commission for the Tsilhquot'in to win that victory but, in retrospect, it was the easy one.

At the dawn of the millennium, British Columbia was still largely unceded territory and subject to First Nations land claims. Many Native peoples chose to negotiate through the provincial government's British Columbia treaty process, which even a former deputy minister of Aboriginal Affairs called "cumbersome, expensive and slow."

As independent as ever, the province's 3,500 Tsilhqot'in people chose a different path. They sought compensation and legal ownership, not through violence, as their war chief Klatsassin had, nor through the provincial government's treaty process. In 2002, the Tsilhqot'in sought land rights through litigation. The small Xeni Gwet'in band brought legal action against the province in a 5-year, 339-day trial that eventually cost $28 million.

In a 2007 landmark ruling running almost 500 pages, the BC Supreme Court "recognized" the Tsilhqot'in's aboriginal title to about half of the 444,000-hectare traditional territory, but stopped short of a formal declaration. The ruling was overturned on a provincial government appeal.

On June 26, 2014, the Supreme Court of Canada upheld the 2007 BC Supreme Court decision. In a unanimous ruling, the federal court granted aboriginal title to 1,700 square kilometres of land traditionally held by the Natives. However, the court declared that title was not absolute. Economic development could still proceed on land where title was established (as it was in this case)—as long as the development had the consent of the First Nation. One hundred and fifty years after Klatsassin and his followers faced the hangman as "murderers," Tsilhqot'in and other Native peoples celebrated the findings of 21st-century justice.

Grand Chief Stewart Phillip, president of the Union of BC Indian Chiefs, Chief Roger William, who brought the case, and other Tsilhqot'in chiefs were sitting together when they learned of the top court's decision. "The room just erupted in cheers and tears," Phillip told CBC News that day. "Everybody is absolutely jubilant. It's very emotional."

* * *

Above the head of Bute Inlet, nothing remains of Alfred Waddington's dream, although a 21st-century road appears to follow a part of his doomed route into the Coast Mountains.

Six years after Waddington's death, the Canadian government chose the Fraser River–Burrard Inlet route for the railway, and Bute Inlet faded into obscurity again. Climate and isolation later defeated farmers. In the late 1920s, the Homathko River was investigated for hydro power, but more accessible waterways were chosen. In 1976, an Okanagan College expedition exploring future recreation possibilities admitted it "grossly underestimated the severity of the conditions" and concluded the inlet was too remote to develop canoeing, mountaineering or backpacking tourism.

Today, Bute Inlet is still the home of the Homalco people, as it has been for generations. Nowadays, between May and November, Native eco-tour guides welcome hundreds of big-city bear-watchers who fly in to visit Grizzly Country.

Selected Bibliography

Dozens of published and unpublished materials were consulted in the preparation of this book. The following are the sources I found most indispensable.

Books and Articles

Brown, Lundin R.C. *Klatsassan: And Other Reminiscences of Missionary Life in British Columbia*. London: Tract Committee, Society for Promoting Christian Knowledge, 1873.

Hume, Stephen. *Simon Fraser: In Search of Modern British Columbia*. Madeira Park, BC: Harbour Publishing, 2008.

Mole, Rich. "Amor De Cosmos," *Times Colonist*, September 28, October 5, 12 and 19, 2008.

Paterson, T.W. *British Columbia: The Pioneer Years*, Vol. 1. Langley, BC: Stagecoach Publishing Company Ltd., 1980.

Pethick, Derek. *Victoria: The Fort*. Vancouver: Mitchell Press Ltd., 1968.

Rothenburger, Mel. *The Chilcotin War*. Langley, BC: Mr. Paperback, 1978.

_____ . *The Wild McLeans*. Victoria: Orca Book Publishers, 1993.

Turkel, William J. *The Archive of Place, Unearthing the Pasts of the Chilcotin Plateau*. Vancouver: UBC Press, 2007.

Waddington, Alfred. *The Fraser Mines Vindicated, or, the History of Four Months*. Victoria: Paul de Garro, 1858. Reprint, Vancouver: Private Press of Robert R. Reid, 1949.

Whymper, Frederick. *Travel and Adventure in the Territory of Alaska*. New York: Harper and Brothers, 1871.

Wright, Ronald. *What Is America?* Toronto: Alfred A. Knopf Canada, 2008.

Newspapers

British Colonist (Victoria)
British Columbian (New Westminster)
Daily Chronicle (Victoria)

Website

"We Do Not Know His Name: Klatsassin and the Chilcotin War." Great Unsolved Mysteries in Canadian History. http://www.canadianmysteries.ca.

Unpublished Sources

Begbie, Matthew Baillie. "Notes on Proceedings, British Columbia Supreme Court, Quesnellemouth, Sept. 1864." Matthew Baillie Begbie Fonds, Provincial Archives of British Columbia.

Tiedeman, H.O. "Report to Waddington, July 1862." Typescript. Provincial Archives of British Columbia.

Index

Index

About the Author

Rich Mole is a former broadcaster, communications consultant and president of a Vancouver Island advertising agency. Fuelled by a lifelong fascination with history, he writes extensively about the events and people of Canada's past. Rich lives in Chilliwack, where he continues to write fiction. He welcomes readers' emailed comments at rich_mole@yahoo.com.

More Amazing Stories by Rich Mole

Scoundrels and Saloons: Whisky Wars of the Pacific Northwest, 1840–1917

print ISBN 978-1-927051-78-8
ebook ISBN 978-1-927051-79-5

Bootleggers, temperance crusaders and big business struggle for control of the liquor trade in frontier settlements of the Pacific Northwest.

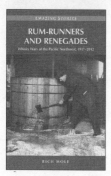

Rum-runners and Renegades: Whisky Wars of the Pacific Northwest, 1917–2012

print ISBN 978-1-927527-25-2
ebook ISBN 978-1-927527-26-9

An action-filled account of liquor and lawlessness on the West Coast.

Visit heritagehouse.ca to see the entire list of books in this series.